MW00415370

PALM BEACH

PALM BEACH

THE ESSENTIAL GUIDE
TO AMERICA'S LEGENDARY RESORT TOWN

RICK ROSE

PHOTOGRAPHS BY MISSY JANES

Globe
Pequot

GUILFORD, CONNECTICUT

Globe Pequot

An imprint of Rowman & Littlefield

Distributed by NATIONAL BOOK NETWORK

Copyright © 2017 by Rick Rose

Unless otherwise noted, photos by Missy Janes

Additional photo credits:
Historical Society of Palm Beach County
Discover the Palm Beaches
Greg Lovett
Glenn Weiss
Michael Ridgdill
Mario Lombardo

British Library Cataloguing in Publication Information Available
Library of Congress Cataloging-in-Publication Data Available

ISBN 978-1-4930-2889-4 (paperback)
ISBN 978-1-4930-2890-0 (e-book)

∞™ The paper used in this publication meets the minimum requirements of American National Standard for Information Sciences—Permanence of Paper for Printed Library Materials, ANSI/NISO Z39.48-1992

In memory of my friend, teacher, and mentor
James Augustine Ponce

CONTENTS

Introduction: America's First Resort Destination

Palm Beach lays claim to the title "America's First Resort Destination" because it was the first purpose-built destination in the United States developed solely for leisure travelers. Although the banks of the Lake Worth Lagoon were already dotted with pioneer settlers and the popular Coconut Grove House was housing seasonal guests each winter in the early 1880s, the area didn't really take off as a winter haven for northerners until the industrial magnate Henry Morrison Flagler, cofounder of Standard Oil, discovered the Lake Worth region in the early 1890s. Flagler, purportedly enchanted by the tropical vegetation and thousands of coconut palms along the banks of the lagoon, was searching for a location to build a hotel where northerners could escape freezing temperatures. The sensitive tropical vegetation was a good indication that the area rarely, if ever, had frost.

Ironically, coconut palms (*Cocos nucifera*) are not indigenous to Florida. They were brought here when the cargo ship *Providencia* ran aground off the shores of current-day Palm Beach in 1878 and the crew and cargo of 20,000 coconuts were rescued by local pioneer families. The locals kept the valuable coconuts and created Florida's first coconut grove along the banks of the Lake Worth Lagoon.

The settlement became known as Palm Beach, and it was the perfect location to fulfill Flagler's vision to build one of America's grandest Gilded Age hotels, the Hotel Royal Poinciana, which opened in 1894. Enlarged twice and doubled in size each time, it became the largest wooden structure in the world (as reported by multiple historians) with 1,700 employees and accommodations for 2,000 guests. Flagler completed the Florida East Coast Railway to Palm Beach in 1896 and the Hotel Royal Poinciana became the preeminent winter destination for the wealthy elite, the only socioeconomic class able to afford to travel for leisure during the Gilded Age.

As the growing affluent class of professionals and successful merchants began to travel in the early 20th century, summer destinations such as Newport, Rhode Island; the Hamptons, New York; the Berkshires in Massachusetts

Standard Oil cofounder Henry Morrison Flagler was so enchanted by tropical Palm Beach that he created what is now the Breakers as a destination for notherners to escape frigid winters. Photo courtesy of the Historical Society of Palm Beach County

and several others also became popular. However, in the winter, Palm Beach remained the primary, most important destination in the continental United States for the next quarter century, resulting in a remarkable concentration of wealth and power on the 11-mile-long island during "the Season"—between Christmas and Easter.

To meet the demand, Flagler built a second hotel, which would eventually become the famous Breakers Hotel. Although other winter destinations have since emerged, Palm Beach remains the preeminent exclusive winter resort destination for America's "moneyed aristocracy." Palm Beach's 33480 zip code often tops the list of America's wealthiest zip codes in terms of average income and household net worth.

TRANSITION FROM A RESORT TO A TOWN

Palm Beach was still mainly a resort in the early 1900s, with a few residences and a short season (Jan 2 to Feb 22). As the resort expanded in capacity, the community prospered and incorporated into a town in 1911. The incorporation of the town was also prompted by, at least in part, the desire to prevent the nearby City of West Palm Beach from incorporating Palm Beach Island into its city limits. Palm Beachers wanted the right to govern themselves.

Furthermore, heightened political tensions in Europe, leading up to and during World War I, affected the travel habits of wealthy Americans, many of whom had vacationed in or built residences on the European Riviera over the previous century. With that region less accessible, Americans began to look to Palm Beach as an alternative. The destination was developing into the American Riviera.

ARRIVAL OF PARIS SINGER AND ADDISON MIZNER

Paris Singer, an heir to the Singer Sewing Machine fortune, was one of the Americans ejected from Europe by the war. He was a man of luxury and a visionary who recognized the potential of Palm Beach. To his friend, architect Addison Mizner, Paris was quoted as saying, "If we start things off right, it will make Palm Beach the winter capital of the world. There is no place in Europe to compare with the climate: All that is needed is to make it gay and attractive. It's up to you and me."

In 1918 Singer decided to build a private club, and he selected Mizner to do the design work. Although highly criticized by the architects of the day because of its eclectic design, the Everglades Club was a huge success. Impressed by the charming Mediterranean Revival design that Mizner had created,

The Royal Poinciana Hotel, the original home of the signature Palm Beach sunset cocktail hour, is pictured here 3 years after Henry Flagler opened its doors in 1894.
Photo courtesy of The Historical Society of Palm Beach County

The Vanderbilts arrived in the first train at the Royal Poinciana Hotel on March 14, 1896. Pictured above, from left: Col. Philip M. Lydig; Miss Helen Morton (Mrs. Morton); Miss Gladys Vanderbilt (Countess Szechenyi) sitting; Miss Amy Townsend; Capt. Rose (Hat & Shoulder); Mrs. Cornelius Vanderbilt (Alice) front; Miss Edith Bishop (Mrs. Moses Taylor) Back-head turned; Miss Mabel Gerry (Mrs. Saxham Drury) black dress; Mrs. Thomas Cushing (Derby); Mr. Edward Livingston; Mr. Dudley Winthrop (between two men); Mr. Craig Wadsworth (standing sidewise); Miss Gertrude Vanderbilt (Mrs. Payne Whitney); Mr. Lispenard Stewart; Mr. Harry Payne Whitney; Miss Sybil Sherman (Mrs. Sellar); Mr. Cornelius Vanderbilt. Photo courtesy of The Historical Society of Palm Beach County

The Bal de Poudre at the Flagler house in 1903 celebrated Washington's birthday. The Washington Birthday Ball became known as the last soiree of the season in the next decades. Photo courtesy of The Historical Society of Palm Beach County

This view of the Everglades Club with historic yachts is from a dock that is no longer there. Photo courtesy of The Historical Society of Palm Beach County

Legendary architect Addison Mizner created the Mediterranean Revival design that defines southern Florida and always kept great company. He is pictured here with his famous pet spider monkey. Photo courtesy of The Historical Society of Palm Beach County

many of the club's wealthy members commissioned him to build their residences in Palm Beach, establishing Mediterranean Revival as one of the most dominant architectural styles.

By the end of the 1920s, Mizner had become the best-known living American architect because of his successes in Palm Beach. Many famous architects from all over the world have made their mark in Palm Beach, including Maurice Fatio, Marion Sims Wyeth, Joseph Urban, Howard Major, and John Volk. Today, there are more than 280 landmarked buildings in the town of Palm Beach and numerous landmarks throughout Palm Beach County, including sixteen historic districts in the City of West Palm Beach, most of which are listed on the National Register of Historic Places.

Although the town of Palm Beach on Palm Beach Island continues to be America's most exclusive winter resort destination as envisioned by Flagler, Singer, and many other influential residents, Palm Beach County has become a diverse community with roughly 1.4 million mostly-year-round residents. The county, which is one of the largest counties east of the Mississippi River, boasts 37 municipalities, many of which use the words Palm Beach in their incorporated titles, such as the towns of Palm Beach and South Palm Beach, the cities of West Palm Beach and Palm Beach Gardens, and the villages of North Palm Beach and Royal Palm Beach. Locals typically refer to the area as "the Palm Beaches."

With over seven million visitors a year and deep historical roots in the hospitality industry, Palm Beach County has become one of the most desirable vacation destinations in the United States, offering visitors from all socioeconomic backgrounds a wide variety of world-class cultural, social, sporting, and commercial venues as well as miles of pristine beaches and beautiful nature.

This guide focuses on the primary destinations of the town of Palm Beach, West Palm Beach, and the nearby surroundings.

Local Lingo

As a proud community with rich local heritage, Palm Beach has a distinctive terminology to best get a point across. Here is the most common lingo found in Palm Beach.

THE PALM BEACHES: The entire Palm Beach County area

THE SEASON: Christmas to Easter

THE ISLAND: Palm Beach Island

PALM BEACH CASUAL: Smart casual attire, which in Palm Beach during the Season typically means loafers, often white or bright pants, and colorful sports coats for men and light/cheery dresses or nice slacks and tops (or light jackets) for women.

THE AVENUE: Worth Avenue

WALKER: A gentleman who accompanies society ladies, usually to a gala or benefit

B & T: Bath and Tennis Club

THE LAKE WORTH LAGOON: Intracoastal Waterway

THE LAKE: Intracoastal Waterway

OTB: Over the Bridge

THE NORTH BRIDGE: The Henry Flagler Memorial Bridge

THE MIDDLE BRIDGE: The Royal Park Bridge

THE SOUTHERN BRIDGE: The Marjorie Merriweather Post Memorial Causeway

OFF THE ISLAND (OTI): Anywhere in Palm Beach County that is not on Palm Beach Island

THE GOLD COAST: Palm Beach, Broward, and Miami-Dade Counties

THE TREASURE COAST: Martin, St. Lucie, and Indian River Counties

Useful Travel Information

WEATHER INFORMATION

Palm Beach, the easternmost town on the Florida peninsula, protrudes into the warm Gulf Stream and has a climate classified as a tropical rainforest on the Köppen climate classification scale. Although there is no official wet or dry season, locals refer to November through April as their dry season and May through October as the wet season. The average annual precipitation is 61 inches (1,500 mm), most of which occurs during the summer season of May through October. As a general rule, when visiting in the winter, a sweater for the evenings is recommended (if you're not already wearing a jacket). When visiting in the summer, the lightest, coolest clothing possible is preferred, but a light sweater is still often needed for well air-conditioned restaurants and theaters.

Average Monthly Air Temperatures (°F)

	JAN	FEB	MAR	APR	MAY	JUN	JUL	AUG	SEP	OCT	NOV	DEC
High	75	76	79	82	86	89	90	90	88	85	80	76
Low	57	59	62	66	71	74	76	76	75	72	66	60

Average Monthly Ocean Temperatures (°F)

JAN	FEB	MAR	APR	MAY	JUN	JUL	AUG	SEP	OCT	NOV	DEC
74	74	76	78	80	83	84	86	85	83	79	76

Average Monthly Rainfall (inches)

JAN	FEB	MAR	APR	MAY	JUN	JUL	AUG	SEP	OCT	NOV	DEC
3.1	2.9	4.6	3.7	4.5	8.3	5.8	8	8.3	5.1	4.8	3.4

TRANSPORTATION INFORMATION

Getting to the Palm Beaches

BY PLANE

Palm Beach International Airport
1000 James L. Turnage Blvd., West Palm Beach, FL 33415; (561) 471-7400; pbia.org

The most convenient airport servicing the Palm Beaches, Palm Beach International Airport offers 16 airlines with direct flights to most major airport hubs along the East Coast, Midwest, Canada, and the Bahamas.

BY TRAIN

Seaboard Railway Station (West Palm Beach Train Station)

209 S. Tamarind Ave., West Palm Beach, FL 33401; (800) 872-7245 or
(800) 874-7245 (Tri-Rail); amtrak.com

Located in downtown West Palm Beach, both Amtrak (national connections) and Tri-Rail (with South Florida connections) provide service at this station, which was built in 1925 and is listed on the National Register of Historic Places. Tri-Rail offers convenient connections to both Ft. Lauderdale International Airport (FLL) and Miami International Airports (MIA).

West Palm Beach Brightline Station

501 Evernia St., West Palm Beach, FL 33401; gobrightline.com

Located in downtown West Palm Beach, Brightline Station offers higher-speed, intercity express train service connecting the city centers of West Palm Beach, Ft. Lauderdale (30 minutes), and Miami (1 hour). Eventually, Orlando will also be serviced.

Getting Around the Palm Beaches

PUBLIC TRANSPORTATION

The Palm Tran

(561) 841-4200; discover.pbcgov.org/palmtran

The public transportation network of buses connects with the rest of Palm Beach County.

Downtown West Palm Beach Trolley Service

downtownwpb.com/trolley

Downtown West Palm Beach offers a free trolley service for visitors to get around downtown, Northwood, and the Palm Beach Outlets Mall. There are three lines that run 7 days a week at various times and stop at a number of locations downtown. Check out the website for complete information.

TAXI SERVICES

Palm Beach Yellow Cab

(561) 721-2222

Yellow Cab of West Palm Beach

(561) 777-7777

UBER AND LYFT

Both popular apps are widely available throughout the Palm Beach area.

The downtown West Palm Beach Brightline Train Station will offer a new gateway to Palm Beach County. Photo courtesy of Brightline

LIMOUSINE SERVICES

Park Limousine
(800) 462-9929 or (561) 832-2222; parklimo.net

Park Limousine is a family-run business based on Palm Beach Island since 1978. It owns 60 vehicles that serve Palm Beach, Broward, and Dade Counties as well as offering long-distance trips in and out of the state.

Palm Beach Tours & Transportation
(561) 203-0404; pbtt.com

Based in West Palm Beach with a well-maintained fleet of limousines and luxury sedans, Palm Beach Tours also offers group and event transportation for Palm Beach, Broward, and Dade Counties.

West Palm Beach Limos
(561) 209-1674; limowestpalmbeachfl.com

Based in West Palm Beach with a fleet of luxury sedans, limousines, and SUVs, West Palm Beach Limos primarily services the central Palm Beach County area, but also offers transfers to Miami and Ft. Lauderdale Airports.

BIKE SHARING AND TOURING

SkyBike
(561) 412-1643; skybikewpb.com

Bike kiosks are located throughout the area. SkyBikes are equipped with locks, so you can keep your bike with you as long as you want as you start and stop. Be aware that the meter keeps ticking until you return the bike to an official bike kiosk. At some point, the meter jumps to a 24-hour rate (which is reasonable). The mobile device app is free.

Palm Beach Attire

As the preeminent exclusive winter resort destination in the United States, Palm Beach is dressier than other South Florida and Caribbean resorts, especially during the Season. In the winter and spring, jackets are required or at least recommended for men at many restaurants and social gatherings on the island.

For the finest restaurants and private social gatherings, such as cocktail parties at a private home or at a well-heeled fund-raiser, jackets and ties for men and cocktail dresses for women are appropriate. Major galas are typically black tie or at least semiformal (black tie optional).

Bright and light colors are embraced for both men and women. Think Lilly Pulitzer. White is always fashionable, especially white pants (also for men). The old saying "You don't wear white between Labor Day and Memorial Day, except in Palm Beach" now applies to all of South Florida. Here is a short guide to help you decode Palm Beach fashion etiquette.

WHITE TIE: Black tailcoats and white ties for men, full-length gowns for women. Very rare for Palm Beach.

BLACK TIE: Tuxedo for men and full-length gowns for women. In some cases, an elegant cocktail dress that has a rich color (black, dark blue) might be sufficient, especially if dressed up with opulent jewelry. Very common for major galas.

FORMAL OR BLACK TIE OPTIONAL: A tuxedo isn't required, but the event is still formal enough for one to be appropriate. Men should wear a tuxedo or a formal dark suit and tie. Women should wear a long dress, a dressy suit, or a formal cocktail-length dress in a dark, neutral tone such as brown, gray, or black. Very common for major and slightly-less-major galas.

COCKTAIL ATTIRE (SEMIFORMAL): Common for the top restaurants, private parties, and fund-raisers between 6 and 8 p.m. Men wear combinations of slacks, jackets, ties, pocket squares, and loafers with no socks or footsies (socks not visible above the loafer). Women wear festive cocktail-length dresses.

PALM BEACH CHIC: Slightly less formal than cocktail attire, Palm Beach Chic usually means that cocktail attire should include bright Palm Beach colors (white, pastels, pink, yellow, green, peach, and

Bright, tropical colors and patterns exemplify Palm Beach style.

so on) and typically lighter materials (linens, silks, cottons). Lilly Pulitzer styles are perfect here! Very common for fundraisers, private parties, and fine dining restaurants.

PALM BEACH CASUAL: Common for everyday activities, such as cocktails at a bar or dinner at a restaurant on the island. Men wear slacks (also bright colors) or nice jeans, blazers, pocket squares, and loafers with no socks or with footsies—but no ties. Women can wear summer dresses or nice slacks and tops (or light jackets). Bright colors welcome! In addition to upscale restaurants in the town of Palm Beach, Palm Beach Casual would be typical at nice cocktail parties and fund-raisers in cities and towns off the island (West Palm Beach, Boca Raton, Palm Beach Gardens, and Jupiter).

CASUAL: Casual in the town of Palm Beach is not the same as casual in other South Florida cities. Both men and women wear pants (khakis or nice jeans), possibly Bermuda shorts, open-collar or polo shirts, and loafers. Shorts would be appropriate only for casual activities off the island.

CHAPTER 1

MUST-SEES & MUST-DOS IN PALM BEACH

Every destination has its "must-see and -do" points of interest. With its unique historic, cultural, architectural, and natural beauty, Palm Beach is no different. For all visitors and residents, here are the five "must-see" things to do on Palm Beach Island (otherwise known as "the Island").

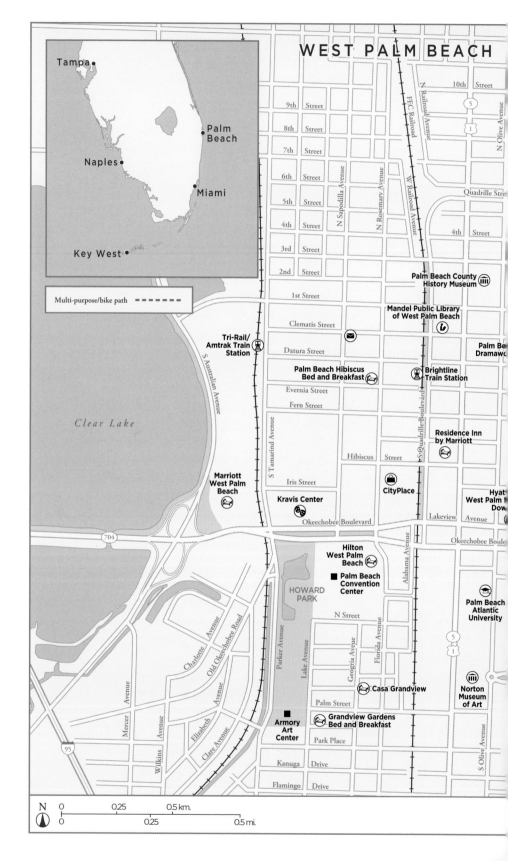

WEST PALM BEACH

Tampa

Palm Beach

Naples

Miami

Key West

Multi-purpose/bike path - - - - - - - -

10th Street

9th Street

8th Street

7th Street

6th Street

5th Street

4th Street

3rd Street

2nd Street

1st Street

Clematis Street

Datura Street

Evernia Street

Fern Street

Hibiscus Street

Iris Street

Okeechobee Boulevard

N Sapodilla Avenue

N Rosemary Avenue

W Railroad Avenue

FEC Railroad

N Railroad Avenue

N Olive Avenue

Quadrille Stre

4th Street

Palm Beach County
History Museum

Mandel Public Library
of West Palm Beach

Palm Be
Dramawc

Tri-Rail/
Amtrak Train
Station

Palm Beach Hibiscus
Bed and Breakfast

Brightline
Train Station

Residence Inn
by Marriott

S Quadrille Boulevard

S Australian Avenue

S Tamarind Avenue

Clear Lake

Marriott
West Palm
Beach

Kravis Center

CityPlace

Hyat
West Palm
Dow

704

Lakeview Avenue

Okeechobee Boule

Hilton
West Palm
Beach

Palm Beach
Convention
Center

HOWARD
PARK

N Street

Alabama Avenue

Palm Beach
Atlantic
University

Charlotte Avenue

Old Okeechobee Road

Parker Avenue

Lake Avenue

Georgia Aveue

Florida Avenue

5
1

Mercer Avenue

Casa Grandview

Norton
Museum
of Art

95

Elizabeth Avenue

Clare Avenue

Wilkins Avenue

Armory
Art
Center

Palm Street

Grandview Gardens
Bed and Breakfast

Park Place

Kanuga Drive

Flamingo Drive

S Olive Avenue

N 0   0.25   0.5 km.
⊕   0.25   0.5 mi.

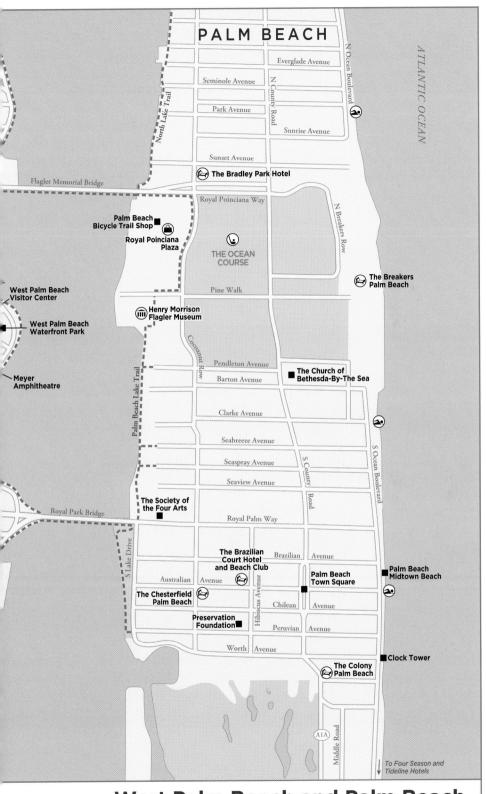

PALM BEACH

Everglade Avenue
Seminole Avenue
Park Avenue
Sunrise Avenue
Sunset Avenue

North Lake Trail
N County Road
N Ocean Boulevard
ATLANTIC OCEAN

The Bradley Park Hotel

Flagler Memorial Bridge

Royal Poinciana Way

N Breakers Row

Palm Beach
Bicycle Trail Shop
Royal Poinciana
Plaza

THE OCEAN
COURSE

The Breakers
Palm Beach

West Palm Beach
Visitor Center

Pine Walk

Henry Morrison
Flagler Museum

West Palm Beach
Waterfront Park

Pendleton Avenue

The Church of
Bethesda-By-The Sea

Meyer
Amphitheatre

Palm Beach Lake Trail
Cocoanut Row

Barton Avenue

Clarke Avenue

Seabreeze Avenue

Seaspray Avenue

Seaview Avenue

S County Road

S Ocean Boulevard

Royal Park Bridge

The Society of
the Four Arts

Royal Palm Way

S Lake Drive

The Brazilian
Court Hotel
and Beach Club

Brazilian   Avenue

Palm Beach
Midtown Beach

Australian   Avenue

Palm Beach
Town Square

The Chesterfield
Palm Beach

Hibiscus Avenue

Chilean   Avenue

Preservation
Foundation

Peruvian   Avenue

Worth   Avenue

Clock Tower

The Colony
Palm Beach

A1A

Middle Road

To Four Season and
Tideline Hotels

West Palm Beach and Palm Beach

Henry Morrison Flagler Museum: Whitehall

One Whitehall Way, Palm Beach, FL 33480; (561) 655-2833; flaglermuseum.us

Designed by acclaimed École des Beaux-Arts–trained architects John Carrère and Thomas Hastings and completed in 1902, this Palm Beach landmark was proclaimed by the *New York Herald* to be "more wonderful than any palace in Europe, grander and more magnificent than any other private dwelling in the world." These architects also collaborated on the design of many other Gilded Age landmarks, including the New York Public Library and the Fifth Avenue mansion of Henry Clay Frick (now the Frick Collection art museum). The immensely wealthy Henry Flagler, cofounder of Standard Oil, built the 75-room, 100,000-square-foot Gilded Age mansion as a wedding present for his wife, Mary Lily Kenan Flagler.

Whitehall, the seasonal Palm Beach home of Henry Morrison Flagler and his wife, Mary Lily Kenan Flagler, is now open to the public as the Henry Morrison Flagler Museum.
Photo courtesy of the Flagler Museum

The couple used the home as a winter retreat from 1902 until Flagler's death in 1913, helping establish the "Palm Beach Season" for the wealthy of the era. Later owners of the property added an 11-story tower with more than 280 guest rooms on the west side and converted the entire structure into a hotel, which operated as such from 1925 to 1959. In 1959, Henry Flagler's granddaughter, Jean Flagler Matthews, learned that the entire structure might be razed and subsequently formed a nonprofit corporation, the Henry Morrison Flagler Museum, to purchase the property. The following year, Whitehall was opened to the public with a grand Restoration Ball on February 6, 1960.

Today, Whitehall is open to the public as the Flagler Museum and is one of only four sites in the nation to be awarded all three of the highest honors given to historic sites: designation as a National Historic Landmark (one of only two in Palm Beach County), accreditation by the American Alliance of Museums, and the Ross Merrill Award for Outstanding Commitment

The Flagler Museum displays the Gilded Age grandeur of Palm Beach.
Photo courtesy of the Flagler Museum

The Flagler Museum displays an exhibit of the original Whitehall drawing room.
Photo courtesy of the Flagler Museum

to the Preservation and Care of Collections. The museum features guided tours, changing exhibits, and special programs. The special programs, which often include live performances, are highly recommended, allowing visitors to experience the ambience of the grand estate more personally. In the winter and spring, the museum opens Café des Beaux-Arts in the Flagler Kenan Pavilion, overlooking the Intracoastal Waterway. Guests are offered an array of delicacies and refreshments reminiscent of the elegance of entertaining during the Gilded Age. The High Tea prix-fixe menu includes a selection of gourmet tea sandwiches, traditional scones, and sweets complemented by the Flagler Museum's own Whitehall Special Blend tea served on exquisite Whitehall Collection china. Designed in the style of a 19th-century Beaux Arts railway palace, the Flagler Kenan Pavilion provides guests with spectacular panoramic views of the West Palm Beach skyline across Lake Worth. Advance purchase is recommended. The price of the afternoon tea includes admission into the museum. Don't miss Flagler's private Railcar No. 91, also located in the pavilion! The museum gift shop has a nice selection of books and gifts relating to Henry Flagler, Palm Beach, and America's Gilded Age.

The museum can be reached by bike using the Palm Beach Lake Trail or by car. There is plenty of parking. Tours of the estate, which are highly recommended, can be booked online and can also be combined with a tour of the Breakers Hotel. Guided tours, audio tours, printed self-guide brochures, and the Flagler Museum Audio App are available and included with admission. Check the website for current tour times and special programs. Open Tuesday through Sunday.

Flagler Museum Music Series

The Flagler family has a long tradition of supporting the performing arts. Henry and Mary Lily Flagler frequently hosted musical performances in Whitehall's elaborate Music Room furnished with a 1,249-pipe J.H. & C.S. Odell & Co. organ and a Steinway upright grand piano. Flagler's son, Henry Harkness Flagler, was chairman of the New York Philharmonic Society. Jean Flagler Matthews, founder of the Flagler Museum, restored Whitehall's elaborate Odell organ and in 1969 brought the New York Philharmonic, conducted by Leonard Bernstein, to South Florida for a Museum benefit concert. Now every winter, guests can experience chamber music in the gracious and intimate setting of the museum's West Room by participating in the Flagler Museum Music Series. Regularly featured on National Public Radio, the highly acclaimed series features performances of music composed prior to 1930. Audience members are treated to a rare opportunity to meet performers during a champagne and dessert reception following each concert.

The Breakers Palm Beach

1 S. County Rd., Palm Beach, FL 33480; (561) 655-6611; thebreakers.com

Listed on the National Register of Historic Places, the Breakers Palm Beach opened on January 16, 1896, as the Palm Beach Inn, occupying the beachfront grounds of the Hotel Royal Poinciana, which had opened two years earlier. Guests began requesting rooms "down by the breakers" (referring to the waves at the beach), so founder Henry Morrison Flagler renamed it the Breakers when the hotel had to be rebuilt after a fire in 1903. Rooms started at $4 per night and included three meals a day. The guest register reads like a who's who of early 20th-century America: Rockefellers, Vanderbilts, Astors, Andrew Carnegie, and J.P. Morgan vacationed alongside US presidents and European nobility.

The Breakers Palm Beach has regally welcomed elite guests for more than a century.

The HMF cocktail bar at the Breakers was named to *Men's Journal*'s "20 Best Hotel Bars in America" for its embodiment of timeless glamour and cool modern nostalgia.

After another fire in 1925, Flagler's heirs were determined to build the grandest hotel in the world as a testament to his vision. Inspired by the Villa Medici in Rome, the Italian Renaissance–style resort opened during the 1926–27 season and was designed by the noted architectural firm Schultze and Weaver, which also designed many famous American landmarks such as Grand Central Station and the Waldorf Astoria in New York City. Seventy-three artisans were brought from Italy to complete the magnificent paintings on the ceilings of the jaw-dropping, 200-foot-long main lobby and first-floor public rooms.

Today, the Breakers Palm Beach is arguably the most exclusive, grandest resort in the world, setting the standard for sophisticated elegance in a tropical resort setting. The sprawling resort boasts lush gardens; shopping; a world-class spa; two highly acclaimed golf courses, including the oldest and first 18-hole course in Florida; and a private beach club with multiple pools.

VISITING THE BREAKERS

When heads of state or other VIPs requiring high security are staying at the resort, it can be difficult to enter the resort without a reservation. With rooms during the Season starting at $700 per night, a visit can get expensive. (Summer rates are much lower and often include complimentary benefits such as dining and golf.) If you are not one of the privileged few to be staying at the hotel, here are a few helpful hints to visit.

Take a Guided Tour

The Flagler Museum conducts weekly tours of the Breakers, either combined with a tour of the Flagler Museum or for the resort alone. During the Season, tours are twice a week on Tuesday and Saturday; during the summer, once a week on Saturday. Tours sell out fast. Go to flaglermuseum.us for more information and to purchase tickets.

Dine at HMF or the Seafood Bar

Named for Henry Morrison Flagler, HMF is not only a good way to see the hotel, it's also a trendy bar and restaurant from which to experience the local scene. Everybody goes here, in particular a young crowd. The restaurant's impressive wine collection anchors the room with 3,000 of the Breakers'

The Breakers Hotel exemplifies Palm Beach glamour.

28,000-bottle collection on display. The overall atmosphere is hip, historic, and sophisticated—all at the same time.

You can also just go for a drink (the cocktails are superb!). Be sure to get your valet ticket validated for complimentary parking. The Seafood Bar restaurant with spectacular views overlooking the ocean is equally impressive. Attire for either in the evening is Palm Beach Chic to Palm Beach Casual. These restaurants are rather expensive, but worth it.

Reserve Sunday Brunch in the Circle

Overlooking the Atlantic in what this well-traveled author considers to be one of the most beautiful dining rooms in the world, the famous Sunday Brunch at the Breakers sets the standard in terms of superior food quality, service, and atmosphere.

In addition to the endless selection of traditional and inventive breakfast dishes, hot lunch items, raw bar selections, in-house prepared pastries, and

Henry Morrison Flagler's heirs determined to build the grandest hotel in the world after damage from a 1925 fire.

flowing champagne, a harpist also strolls from table to table to add to the elegantly residential-style setting.

RICK'S TIPS To ensure your seat at this highly acclaimed venue, advance reservations are strongly recommended, particularly on holidays and during the Season.

Treat Yourself to the Spa

The updated Spa at the Breakers is considered to be world class. It features a relaxed modern style inspired by the calming virtues of the seaside location and the Italian-influenced architecture, with extensive indoor/outdoor amenities and services. A salon area awaits guests who are seeking hair and nail services; while three dedicated lounges and a private, coed courtyard welcome guests who are seeking specialty treatments and customized massages.

RICK'S TIPS Book a quartz massage—a unique treatment given while you rest on a bed of warm, flowing alpha-quartz sand.

Go Shopping!

As you enter the lobby, turn to the right and eventually you'll find a quaint stretch of storefronts that surrounds the picturesque Palm Courtyard. You can also access the courtyard directly from the outside (in case you are in bicycle shorts!). You can find many recognized brands from high fashion and cosmetics to children's apparel and gourmet treats.

RICK'S TIPS Located in the Palm Courtyard, News & Gourmet shop is part gallery and part café where you can buy a gift, get a coffee and a delicious in-house-made pastry, pick up a paper (or a book or magazine), and then sit in the courtyard to soak in the tropical, elegant ambience of the Breakers. This is an outstanding gift shop!

Once Inside

No matter if you are visiting for the day or spending the week, take the time to walk around and admire the magnificent lobby, lush gardens and courtyards, and specialty boutiques. In particular, take a look at the Mediterranean Ballroom (if there's not an event occurring), and definitely try to peek into the Gold Room, a magnificent space in the south wing with murals of Renaissance rulers and explorers of the New World.

Worth Avenue

Hailed as one of the most exclusive boutique shopping districts in the world, Worth Avenue epitomizes Palm Beach Style and is historically significant mainly for two reasons: Addison Mizner built the Everglades Club here and created the eclectic Mediterranean Revival architectural style that became all the rage across Florida and the entire country during the 1910s and 1920s, and Worth Avenue has been (and still is) the launch pad for many famous luxury brands.

Today, the Worth Avenue area is a charming mixed-used district of approximately 200 shops, boutiques, department stores, galleries, and restaurants as well as residences and offices. The Avenue, as it is known, runs east/west from the Atlantic Ocean to the Lake Worth Lagoon. The major luxury brands are typically situated directly on the Avenue. However, to experience Worth Avenue to its fullest, it's important to explore the so-called "Vias," nine pedestrian passageways

Charming design and excellent boutiques welcome visitors to wander Worth Avenue.

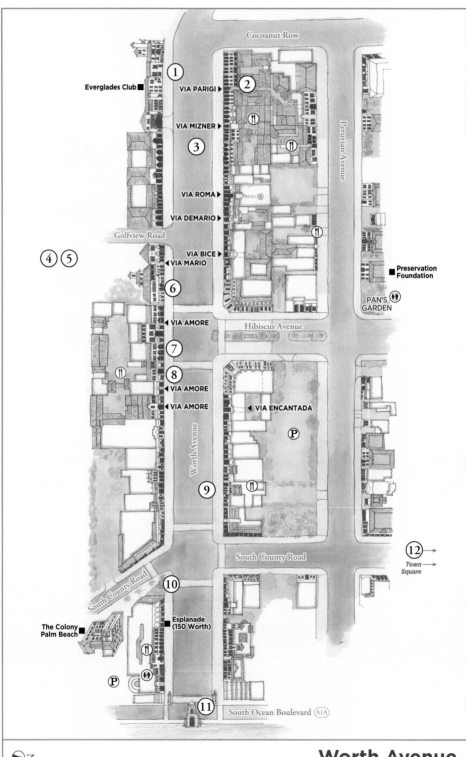

Everglades Club ■

VIA PARIGI ▶

VIA MIZNER ▶

VIA ROMA ▶

VIA DEMARIO ▶

Golfview Road

VIA BICE ▶
◀ VIA MARIO

◀ VIA AMORE

◀ VIA AMORE

◀ VIA AMORE

Cocoanut Row

Peruvian Avenue

Preservation
Foundation ■

PAN'S
GARDEN

Hibiscus Avenue

◀ VIA ENCANTADA

Worth Avenue

South County Road

Town →
Square

South County Road

The Colony
Palm Beach ■

Esplanade ■
(150 Worth)

South Ocean Boulevard (A1A)

N

Worth Avenue

connected to the Avenue on the south and north sides, which lead to pictur-esque interior courtyards. There are additional boutiques, charming gardens, and other points of interest for exploring on nearby Peruvian Avenue and South County Road, especially around Town Square. For more information about current activities and events on Worth Avenue and South County Road, visit worth-avenue.com and gscrapb.org.

TAKE A GUIDED TOUR

Weekly walking tours of Worth Avenue are offered from the beginning of December to the end of April every Wednesday at 11 a.m. The popular tour costs $10, which benefits a local charity chosen each season by the Worth Avenue Association. The tour begins at 256 Worth Ave. (across from Tiffany's), lasts approximately 75 minutes, and covers much of the history of Worth Avenue, including its architectural importance, influence on the fashion world, and the development of the legendary social scene that established Palm Beach as America's first resort destination during the Gilded Age.

DO A SELF-GUIDED TOUR

Many of the most interesting, unique, noncorporate/chain retailers are located in the Vias, nine pedestrian passageways connected to Worth Avenue on the south and north sides. Begin a self-guided tour of the Avenue (which is highly recommended) in the oldest section on the western end near the Everglades Club and work your way to the east (toward the ocean). Starting from this end, the most important points of interest on Worth Avenue are as follows:

THE EVERGLADES CLUB
500 S. County Rd.

Commissioned in 1918 by the immensely wealthy Paris Singer, heir to the Singer Sewing Machine empire, the flamboyant architect Addison Mizner designed the club, which became the catalyst for launching the Mediterranean Revival architectural style and for the creation of Worth Avenue into a luxury retail mile.

The club is still private and visitors are not permitted entry unless accompa-nied by a member. You can best view the club by standing across the street with your back to the entrance of Via Parigi. Looking at the club from left to right, you will notice many types of Mediterranean architectural styles represent-ing different periods and regions. Mizner was attempting to imitate the Old World ambience of the Italian Riviera, where towns date back centuries and have architectural influences from the entire Mediterranean region.

Addison Mizner designed the Everglades Club in the Mediterranean Revival architectural style.

The club members embraced the architectural style, and many of the wealthy members asked Mizner to build their homes in a similar fashion, propagating the Mediterranean Revival style throughout the region. Observe the "pecky cypress" wood beams extending out of the roof line. Insects and decay imparted a distressed look to the wood, yet the wood is sturdy and functional for building. It suited Mizner's needs perfectly, because he strove to make the buildings look much older and "historic" in appearance than they were. You can get a closer look at pecky cypress by viewing the ceilings of the walkway to the left and right of Via Parigi along Worth Avenue.

The Everglades Club proved to be extremely popular with 500 members joining within two years. To improve the offerings for members, Singer and Mizner decided to develop the infrastructure around the club to include luxury boutiques that could cater to the affluent club members, leading to the birth of the Worth Avenue luxury retail district.

VIA PARIGI
Worth Avenue, between Cocoanut Row and Hibiscus Avenue

Via Parigi is named after Paris Singer (*Parigi* is Italian for Paris). Stroll into the via from Worth Avenue and you'll think you're on one of the back islands of Venice, which was one of Mizner's favorite cities. Continue toward the rear and the via opens to a charming piazza with a fountain and unique boutiques and galleries. It is believed that family members of Mizner lived in the apartment upstairs on the east side with the stained-glass windows.

VIA MIZNER
Worth Avenue, between Cocoanut Row and Hibiscus Avenue

Continue your stroll from the piazza in the rear of Via Parigi and enter Via Mizner directly (you can also enter Via Mizner from Worth Avenue). Listed on the National Register of Historic Places, Via Mizner is notable because this is where Villa Mizner, Addison Mizner's private residence, is located. In addition, many designer brands, including Lilly Pulitzer, trace their roots to this via.

Entering from Worth Avenue, you'll see the tower structure on the left, which is the beautifully restored Villa Mizner, still a private residence. Also on the left, there will be an opening leading into Piazza Torlonia, named after an Italian aristocratic family who had a shop there in earlier times.

Via Parigi is one of nine pedestrian passageways that accentuate the Worth Avenue experience.

The beautifully restored Villa Mizner is still a private residence.

As you enter the piazza, you will see two gravestones in the rear of the charming (and highly recommended) Pizza Al Fresco restaurant. One tombstone is marked "Johnnie Brown, the Human Monkey." Johnnie Brown was Mizner's famous pet spider monkey that contributed to his master's celebrity status. Mizner memorialized his pet by creating the bronze impressions of Johnnie's face that are located over the entrances to the residence.

The second tombstone, inscribed "Our Laddie," is the grave of Mortimer and Rose Sachs' dog, Laddie. The Sachs family lived at Villa Mizner for more than 40 years and buried their beloved family dog next to Johnnie Brown in 1952. Initially the town council did not want to allow the second grave, but after considerable lobbying efforts by the Sachs family, they reversed course and declared this would be the last grave in Palm Beach. So these two graves, one for a monkey and one for a dog, make up the only cemetery in town.

HOGARCITO
17 Golfview Rd.

Around the corner (just off Worth), behind Maus & Hoffman at 312 Worth Ave., you can see the Mediterranean Revival estate "Hogarcito." Commissioned by socialite and cereal heiress Marjorie Merriweather Post and her then husband, E.F. Hutton, it was designed by society architect Marion Sims Wyeth and built in 1921. The estate has been the setting for many famous social gatherings. Please note that this is a private residence best viewed from a distance directly at the entrance to Golfview Road (without actually entering road).

The Hogarcito estate exemplifies Palm Beach's Mediterranean Revival architectural style.

This 1925 estate, La Claridad, remains a private residence.

The courtyard of Via Amore has hosted many an elaborate fashion show.

LA CLARIDAD
16 Golfview Rd.

"La Claridad" was built in 1925 for Clarence Geist, the Philadelphia utilities magnate who went on to purchase Addison Mizner's bankrupt Mizner Development Corporation, which included the lavish Cloister Inn that he expanded and reopened as the Boca Raton Club (today the Boca Raton Resort & Club). Please note that this is a private residence best viewed from a distance directly at the entrance to Golfview Road (without actually entering the road).

300 WORTH AVE.

Now a Ralph Lauren store, this building is particularly notable because it was built as the second Saks Fifth Avenue in 1926 after the first such-named store in New York.

VIA AMORE
256 Worth Ave.

This charming expansive via is nicknamed Via Gucci because Aldo Gucci purchased some of these buildings and introduced many of the new Gucci styles with elaborate fashion shows in the courtyard. Further east in the courtyard, near Café Flora, view the bronze sculptures of children frolicking created by sculptor Prince Monyo, one of the last heirs to the Romanian throne.

KASSATLY'S
250 Worth Ave.

Opened in 1923, this is Worth Avenue's oldest shop, specializing in the ultimate in men's and women's sleepwear as well as fine linens. It is still run by the Kassatly brothers, Edward and Robert.

TA-BOO
221 Worth Ave.

Opened in 1941, just before the country entered World War II, this legendary restaurant has been a favorite watering hole for some of the island's most famous residents and visitors, including John F. Kennedy, Frank Sinatra, the Duke and Duchess of Windsor, Rod Stewart, and James Patterson. The Bloody Mary cocktail was rumored to have been concocted here for the famous socialite Barbara Hutton, who lived just off Worth Avenue.

THE LIVING WALL
Worth Avenue

Deborah Kotalic designed the 840-square-foot vertical garden with 11 different varieties and a total of 10,900 plants on the west wall of Saks Fifth Avenue. The living wall is meant to convey the lush tropical look of palm trees and is one

Ta-boo restaurant has been serving Palm Beach residents and visitors on Worth Avenue since 1941.

The Living Wall is 840 square feet of lush Florida vegetation.

of the many contributions of the influential Garden Club of Palm Beach, which was established in 1928 and created a town plan for public spaces that still acts as a guideline for the area.

THE CLOCK TOWER
Worth Avenue

The 30-foot-tall tower at the east end of Worth Avenue serves as a monument to the Palm Beach Pier that stretched into the Atlantic from 1926 to 1969. This is a great spot to see the ocean and take photos.

TOWN SQUARE

Located on South County Road between Brazilian and Chilean Avenues, just 2 blocks north of Worth Avenue, the focal point of Palm Beach's traditional Town Square is the Memorial Fountain Plaza. Appointed by the Memorial Fountain Commission in 1929, the fountain was designed by legendary architect Addison Mizner and presented to the town by Harold S. Vanderbilt in 1930 "as a gift from its residents" to memorialize the contributions of local pioneers.

This project was Mizner's last commission in Palm Beach. On the upper terrace is a central fountain, inspired by the Fountain of the Sea Horses, an 18th-century work by Christopher Unterberger at the Villa Borghese in Rome.

The Clock Tower on Worth Avenue is a sight in itself.

A World War II memorial plaque was added in 1985. Originally built in 1925, the Palm Beach Town Hall, located on the south side of the square, was designed by noted local architects Harvey & Clarke and is individually listed on the National Register of Historic Places.

Memorial Fountain Plaza is the center of Palm Beach's Town Square.

RICK'S TIPS To really experience and appreciate the ambience of this world-renowned, historic luxury boutique shopping district, allow plenty of time to explore and shop and definitely plan on combining your visit with lunch. No visit is complete without lunching at one of the famous restaurants on the Avenue. Although restaurants in Palm Beach tend to be pricey in the evening, lunch menus are notably inexpensive, especially when considering the ambience and quality. While you have lunch, you'll very likely get to see models pass your table wearing some of the finest couture designs or you might even see celebrities or other famous Palm Beach personalities. Plan to arrive on Worth Avenue in the late morning, then tour and shop, and then have lunch. It's one of *the* Palm Beach experiences.

The Lake Trail

In the 1890s, the Lake Trail was the main transportation artery on the island. The main mode of transportation was the Palm Beach Chariot, a type of three-wheeled wicker rickshaw (popular until the late 1950s). Today, no visit to Palm Beach is complete without a walk or bike ride along the gorgeous multipurpose path that winds alongside and through some of the most notable landmarks on the island. You can jump on or off anywhere on the path, which mainly runs along the Lake Worth Lagoon.

The longest section of the trail extends from Royal Poinciana Way to almost the northern tip of the island. The shorter, but more historic section is between Royal Poinciana Way and Royal Palm Way. Many visitors start their tour by renting a bike at Palm Beach Bicycle Trail Shop (50 Cocoanut Row; palmbeach bicycle.com) on the south side of the Royal Poinciana Plaza. Parking is available at the plaza. The staff offers helpful tips and can usually supply a basic map.

The Palm Beach Chariot has fallen out of use, but the Lake Trail is still a favorite route to walk or bike around the island.

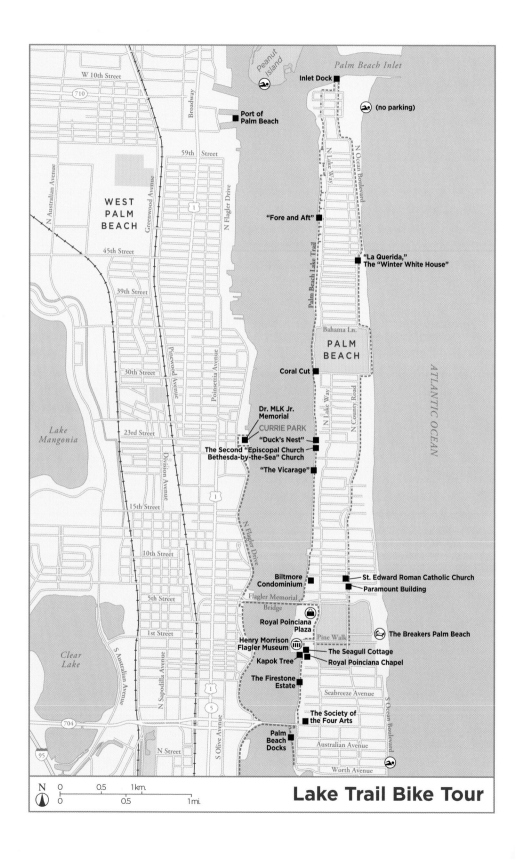

W 10th Street

Broadway

Peanut Island

Palm Beach Inlet

Inlet Dock

(no parking)

Port of Palm Beach

WEST PALM BEACH

N Australian Avenue

Greenwood Avenue

710

59th Street

45th Street

N Flagler Drive

1

N Lake Way

N Ocean Boulevard

"Fore and Aft"

"La Querida," The "Winter White House"

39th Street

Pinewood Avenue

Poinsettia Avenue

30th Street

Bahama Ln.

PALM BEACH

Palm Beach Lake Trail

Lake Mangonia

23rd Street

Coral Cut

Dr. MLK Jr. Memorial

CURRIE PARK

"Duck's Nest"

The Second "Episcopal Church Bethesda-by-the-Sea" Church

"The Vicarage"

N Lake Way

N County Road

Division Avenue

15th Street

1

N Flagler Drive

10th Street

5th Street

Biltmore Condominium

St. Edward Roman Catholic Church

Paramount Building

Flagler Memorial Bridge

Royal Poinciana Plaza

The Breakers Palm Beach

Pine Walk

Clear Lake

1st Street

S Australian Avenue

N Sapodilla Avenue

Henry Morrison Flagler Museum

The Seagull Cottage

Kapok Tree

Royal Poinciana Chapel

1

The Firestone Estate

Seabreeze Avenue

S Ocean Boulevard

704

5

N Street

S Olive Avenue

The Society of the Four Arts

Australian Avenue

95

Palm Beach Docks

Worth Avenue

ATLANTIC OCEAN

N

0   0.5   1km.

0   0.5   1mi.

Lake Trail Bike Tour

Starting the tour from the bike shop, enter the Lake Trail right at the Royal Poinciana Plaza, which at that location runs parallel to Cocoanut Row. If you want to explore the northern section of the island, head north following the path under the Flagler Memorial Bridge. When returning south from the inlet at the north end of the trail, ride on North Ocean Boulevard and then North County Road to enjoy the vistas of the Atlantic Ocean and to see some of the island's most spectacular estates.

RICK'S TIPS Located in the Royal Poinciana Plaza just a few feet from the Palm Beach Bicycle Trail Shop, TooJay's Gourmet Deli is a great place to pick up a sandwich, chips, and drinks for your bike tour. Offering popular menu items such as corned beef, matzo-ball soup, and other Jewish deli favorites, this locally renowned casual restaurant is also great to dine in for lunch or dinner before or after your bike tour.

The Lake Trail Part 1: Heading north of Royal Poinciana Way

ROYAL POINCIANA PLAZA
340 Royal Poinciana Way

Built in 1957 by notable architect John Volk and landmarked by the town of Palm Beach, this is one of the largest examples of commercial Regency architecture in the area. A historic marker along the Lake Trail denotes the significance of the original hotel built here by Henry Flagler. An impressive 11 foot bronze statue of Henry Flagler is situated in the median diagonally across from the plaza just to the east of the Royal Poinciana Way/Cocoanut Row intersection.

BILTMORE CONDOMINIUM
150 Bradley Place

Located just a few hundred feet north of the Flagler Memorial Bridge, the current building was constructed in 1926 and opened as the Spanish-themed Alba Hotel. Biltmore Hotels later took it over before it served as an enlisted women's training center for the US Coast Guard and then a hospital during World War II and again as a luxury hotel after the war. It became an exclusive condominium in 1981.

"THE VICARAGE"
448 N. Lake Way

This icon of pre-Mediterranean Revival architecture was built in 1897 as the home of the vicar of the Episcopal Church of Bethesda-by-the-Sea. Since then, this private residence has had many famous residents, including Douglas Fairbanks Jr.

The second home of the Bethesda Episcopal congregation is now a private residence.

THE SECOND "EPISCOPAL CHURCH BETHESDA-BY-THE-SEA" CHURCH

Known as Bethesda II, this structure was built in 1894 near the original location of the first sanctuary, which was the first church in South Florida. The building, which still looks a lot like a church, is now a private residence.

The Lake Trail winds past some of the most noteworthy Palm Beach landmarks.

"DUCK'S NEST"

545 N. Lake Trail

Built in 1891, this is the oldest house in Palm Beach still used as a residence (and still by the same family who built it!).

Duck's Nest is the oldest house on the island.

CORAL CUT

Landmarked by the town of Palm Beach, Coral Cut is to your right (heading north), exposing the coral ridge, which is the geological base of Palm Beach Island. Continue north on the Lake Trail.

Photo courtesy of Glenn Weiss

FORE AND AFT
1221 N. Lake Way

Acclaimed architect Belford Shoumate built this Art Deco house in 1939. Contemporaries admired the fusion of classic nautical elements with futuristic architecture. Fore and Aft has hosted many famous guests, including the great composer, pianist, and former Prime Minister of Poland, Ignacy Jan Paderewski, who lived at the house during the 1941 Season.

Eventually, the Lake Trail curves around the Palm Beach Sailfish Club, running along the eastern edge of the parking lot and then back around along the water before finally ending just south of Esplanade Way. Turn left off of the Lake Trail on to North Lake Way.

INLET DOCK

Continue north on North Lake Way to Indian Road, turn right and then left on North Ocean Boulevard to find your way to the northern tip of Palm Beach (and the end of North Ocean Boulevard). The Inlet Dock is a great place to rest and watch ships and yachts coming in and out to sea. There is also a fountain for thirsty bikers! To return south, you can either return on the Lake Trail or head back south on North Ocean Boulevard, which leads you along the ocean. The route below is along North Ocean Boulevard.

LA QUERIDA
1095 N. Ocean Blvd.

Joseph P. Kennedy Sr., the Kennedy family patriarch, bought this house in 1933 from the Wanamakers—of Philadelphia department-store fame—for use as a winter retreat for his family, including wife, Rose, and their children. The two-story house was designed by noted society architect Addison Mizner in 1924. Also known as the former Kennedy Estate, the winter home for generations of Kennedys, including President Kennedy, always has been a private residence (and still is today). President Kennedy was said to have worked on his inaugural address here.

ST. EDWARD ROMAN CATHOLIC CHURCH
144 N. County Rd., Palm Beach, FL 33480; (561) 832-0400

Completed in 1926 in the Spanish Renaissance architectural style, with an elaborate interior, St. Edward was the favorite church of many notable Palm Beach Catholic families including the Kennedys.

Notice St. Edward Roman Catholic Church, where the Kennedys worshipped while in town.

President Kennedy in Palm Beach

John Fitzgerald "Jack" Kennedy (May 29, 1917 – November 22, 1963), commonly referred to by his initials JFK, was the 35th president of the United States from January 1961 until his assassination in November 1963. Since the early 1930s, the Kennedy family often stayed in their home on North Ocean Boulevard and were very present in Palm Beach society during the Season, in particular over the Christmas and Easter holidays. At the height of the Cold War leading up to the Cuban missile crisis, the US government built the "Kennedy Bunker," a nuclear fallout shelter for President Kennedy and his family on nearby Peanut Island, an interesting Cold War relic that can be visited today. The Kennedy clan members could be seen shopping on Worth Avenue, dining at local restaurants, and attending local charity events. This tradition continued long after the Kennedy presidency.

PARAMOUNT BUILDING
139 N. County Rd.

Completed in 1927 by the famous architect Joseph Urban, the Paramount Building was hailed at that time as the "Millionaire's Movie Theater," where a balcony box cost $1,000 for the 13-week season. The building, now listed on the National Register of Historic Places, hosted numerous famous performers, including W.C. Fields, George Gershwin, Jack Benny, Danny Kaye, Ed Sullivan, Bob Hope, and Barbra Streisand, before becoming an office building.

The Lake Trail Part 2: South of Royal Poinciana Way

If you are continuing the tour from the north end, you can bike or walk south on North County Road until the entrance of the Breakers. Beware that there is no official bike path along North County Road from roughly Wells Road to the south through the Breakers grounds, so stay to the right (or use the sidewalk). About 150 feet beyond the entrance of the hotel (to the south), on your right there is a small road called Pine Walk that you can use to get back to the Lake Trail at the Flagler Museum.

FLAGLER MUSEUM, WHITEHALL (ONE WHITEHALL WAY)

Henry Flagler's estate, built in 1902, is now a museum. See detailed information about the estate museum on page 4.

THE SEAGULL COTTAGE

Built in 1886 by R.R. McCormick in the typical architectural style of the lake region of that time, this is the oldest house in Palm Beach and was at one point Henry Flagler's winter residence while Whitehall was being built. There is a historic marker on the trail.

ROYAL POINCIANA CHAPEL

Built in 1898, the Royal Poinciana Chapel was largely financed by Flagler, who insisted it be nondenominational (Christian) to serve the needs of his many hotel guests. The chapel is also a great stop to make on the return from regional driving tours.

KAPOK TREE

At the western side of the Royal Poinciana Chapel gardens adjacent to the Lake Trail, the magnificent kapok tree (*Ceiba pentandra*) dates to the mid-1800s and is nicknamed the "dinosaur tree" by children due to the enormous exposed roots. The tree has been a Palm Beach landmark since the Flagler era. With views to the West Palm Beach skyline, this is one of the most popular locations to take photos in the entire Palm Beach area.

THE FIRESTONE ESTATE

8 S. Lake Tr.

Commissioned by the Firestone family as their Palm Beach residence, this 10,000-square-foot estate was built by architect John Volk in 1937.

The enormous kapok tree is visible from the Lake Trail.

SOCIETY OF THE FOUR ARTS

2 Four Arts Plaza, Palm Beach, FL 33480; (561) 655-7227; fourarts.org

The Society of the Four Arts has provided quality cultural programming to the resort community for more than 80 years. The Four Arts Botanical Gardens and Philip Hulitar Sculpture Garden are beautiful, peaceful spots for a break and a view. You'll find more information about the Society of the Four Arts on page 63.

PALM BEACH DOCKS

Located along the most southern portion of the Lake Trail, south of the Royal Park Bridge, these docks offer a close look at some of the most beautiful yachts in the world.

The Society of the Four Arts gardens and sculpture gardens are beautiful and peaceful.

The Palm Beach Loop: A Self-Guided Scenic Driving Tour

A driving tour of Palm Beach to see famous mansions, gardens, and vistas of the Atlantic and the Lake Worth Lagoon (Intracoastal Waterway) is one of the most popular activities for visitors who have a car. A tour can be half a day or only 30 minutes, depending on how much time you have and what you want to see. You definitely want to take this tour during daylight hours, and it's highly recommended to drive the A1A/ ocean part of your tour from south to north to have a better view of the estates and not be blinded by the sun.

With no stops, the complete recommended tour takes about 45 to 60 minutes and includes the eastern edge of the City of West Palm Beach so you can enjoy the views of Palm Beach from the west side of the lagoon. However, the tour can be shortened by excluding the southern half of the "loop," which includes the City of Lake Worth as well as the so-called "Billionaire's Row" in the southern part of the town of Palm Beach. The itinerary below includes the section of the loop that can be excluded to shorten your tour.

Luxury cars add to the glamourous tour of Palm Beach.

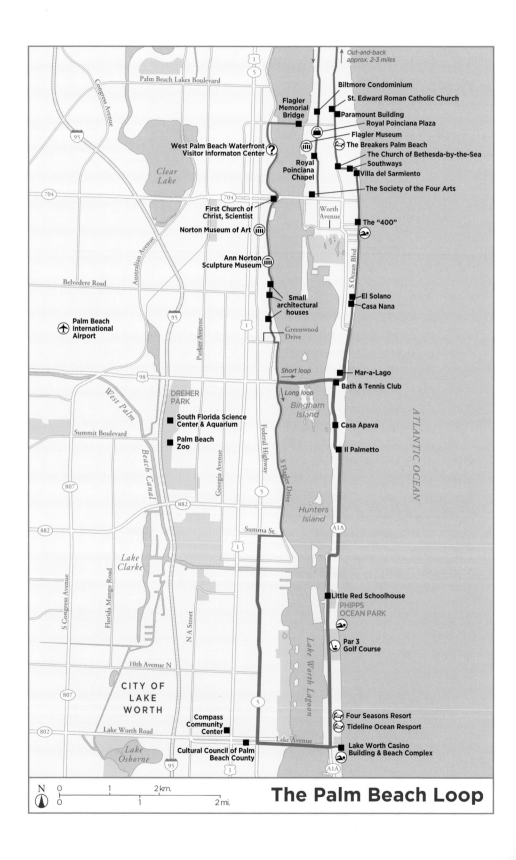

The Palm Beach Loop

Out-and-back
approx. 2-3 miles

Biltmore Condominium
St. Edward Roman Catholic Church
Flagler Memorial Bridge
Paramount Building
Royal Poinciana Plaza
Flagler Museum
The Breakers Palm Beach
The Church of Bethesda-by-the-Sea
Southways
Villa del Sarmiento
The Society of the Four Arts

West Palm Beach Waterfront Visitor Informaton Center
Royal Poinciana Chapel

First Church of Christ, Scientist
Norton Museum of Art

The "400"

Ann Norton Sculpture Museum

El Solano
Casa Nana

Small architectural houses

Greenwood Drive

Palm Beach International Airport

Short loop

Mar-a-Lago
Bath & Tennis Club

Long loop

Bingham Island

Casa Apava

Il Palmetto

DREHER PARK

South Florida Science Center & Aquarium

Palm Beach Zoo

Summit Boulevard

Hunters Island

Summa St.

Lake Clarke

Little Red Schoolhouse
PHIPPS OCEAN PARK

Par 3 Golf Course

CITY OF LAKE WORTH

Lake Worth Lagoon

10th Avenue N

Compass Community Center

Four Seasons Resort
Tideline Ocean Resort

Lake Worth Road

Lake Osborne

Cultural Council of Palm Beach County

Lake Worth Casino Building & Beach Complex

Palm Beach Lakes Boulevard

Congress Avenue

Clear Lake

Belvedere Road

Australian Avenue

Parker Avenue

Georgia Avenue

West Palm Beach Canal

Beach Canal

Federal Highway

S Flagler Drive

Florida Mango Road

N A Street

S Congress Avenue

Lake Avenue

ATLANTIC OCEAN

S Ocean Blvd

Worth Avenue

N   0   1   2 km.
     0   1   2 mi.

Assuming you are beginning in the town of Palm Beach, head west over the Flagler Memorial Bridge (north bridge) and turn south (left) onto Flagler Drive in West Palm Beach. You will be heading south on Flagler Drive, enjoying panoramic views across the Intracoastal Waterway to Palm Beach as you drive through downtown, and eventually enter residential areas. When you reach Southern Boulevard, you can turn left and cross the bridge back to Palm Beach and then head north along A1A, or you can continue south for the longer version of this tour.

Turning onto Flagler Drive from the Flagler Memorial Bridge (north bridge), here are the main points of interest:

WEST PALM BEACH

You will find a more extensive chapter about visiting West Palm Beach on page 70, but on your scenic driving tour, you can pass through downtown or stop at the Waterfront Park at the east end of Clematis Street for 20 to 30 minutes. You can park your car on the street with metered parking or in one of the parking garages in the immediate vicinity.

For a short stop, stroll along the water and out to the end of the main public dock for panoramic views to Palm Beach and the West Palm Beach skyline. The West Palm Beach Visitors Center, located on the downtown Waterfront Park, can provide information about current events and ticket booking for the fantastic sunset cruise and other water sports activities and excursions. Or call (561) 659-8814 in advance.

Glance across the water to the city of West Palm Beach.

For a quick tour of downtown, hop on a complimentary trolley (daily, year-round). For a longer stop in West Palm Beach, you may wish to rent a bike from SkyBike to get a more extensive look at downtown.

FIRST CHURCH OF CHRIST, SCIENTIST, IN WEST PALM BEACH
809 S. Flagler Dr.

Continue your drive south along Flagler Drive. Located in front of the Royal Park Bridge (the middle bridge), this grand building was built in 1928 in the Classical Revival style. It was designed by Horace Trumbauer, who is considered to be one of the most important American architects from the Gilded Age. Julian Abele, recognized as the first major African American architect in the United States and who was the chief designer for Mr. Trumbauer, also is said to have worked on the design of this church.

Trumbauer designed many famous American landmarks, such as the Philadelphia Museum of Art and the Harry Elkins Widener Memorial Library, the main library of Harvard University. This church has been declared eligible to be individually listed on the National Register of Historic Places.

The First Church of Christ, Scientist, was built in 1928 in the Classical Revival style.

The Norton Museum is the largest fine art museum in Florida.

NORTON MUSEUM OF ART

1451 S. Olive Ave., West Palm Beach, FL 33401; (561) 832-5196; norton.org

Although the address is on South Olive Avenue, the lawn in front of the original entrance to the museum extends east to Flagler Drive, creating an impressive view of the Art Deco/Neoclassical building designed by notable architect Marion Sims Wyeth. The largest fine art museum in Florida, the Norton Museum of Art is one of the most important cultural mainstays in Palm Beach County. The museum is currently undergoing a monumental expansion, led by the internationally acclaimed Lord Norman Foster. The Museum will remain open during this exciting transformation, and "the New Norton" will make its dramatic debut with its new entrance on South Dixie Highway in 2018. For more information about the museum, go to page 67.

EL CID, PROSPECT PARK & SOUTHLAND PARK HISTORIC DISTRICTS

Heading south on Flagler Drive, shortly after the Norton Museum, you will enter into the El Cid Historic District, a residential district facing the lagoon with some of the most noteworthy private historic residences in West Palm Beach dating back to the early 1920s. The tour continues south also through the Prospect Park and Southland Park Historic Districts, as detailed below.

2051 S. FLAGLER DR.

The Ann Norton Sculpture Garden is a 1.7-acre tribute to the artist's life and work. Ann Norton, widow of Ralph Hubbard Norton, lived and created in this residence (now museum) designed by Maurice Fatio. There is more information about this museum and gardens on page 68.

2433 S. FLAGLER DR.

This is one of the finest examples of Mediterranean Revival in West Palm Beach. Numerous prominent residents have resided in this 5,500-square-foot 1925 villa, including a former mayor of West Palm Beach.

2631 S. FLAGLER DR.

This 9,200-square-foot 1937 home built by noted architect Belford Shoumate is one of the finest examples of Art Deco Revival architecture in West Palm Beach.

PROSPECT PARK HISTORIC DISTRICT

Continuing south, where Flagler Drive curves away from the waterfront, the street name changes to Washington Road, and you enter the Prospect Park Historic District. Named after Prospect Park in Brooklyn, New York, the neighborhood boasts a high concentration of 1920s architecture.

3001 WASHINGTON RD.

At the corner of Westminster Road, the 1926 Mediterranean Revival–style home at 3001 Washington Rd. has been meticulously restored by local noted architect Raphael Saladrigas, AIA, and is known for its unique, dominant staircase turret and Oriental/Moorish-influenced porte cochère roofline.

SOUTHLAND PARK HISTORIC DISTRICT

Continue south on Washington Road and when you reach the second stop sign, at Greenwood Drive, you will have made it to the heart of the Southland Park Historic District. Turn left on Greenwood Drive, drive 1 block to the waterfront, and then turn right and head south on the southern section of Flagler Drive to Southern Boulevard.

SHORTER PALM BEACH LOOP TOUR

To shorten your driving tour by about 25 minutes, turn left at Southern Boulevard and cross the Marjorie Merriweather Post Memorial Causeway, named in honor of the prominent American socialite and founder of General Foods, Inc. Mrs. Post (1887–1973) married E.F. Hutton, with whom she had a daughter, actress Dina Merrill. Post became the wealthiest woman in the world and one of the most famous, prominent residents in Palm Beach's history. Her namesake causeway crosses over Bingham Island, a designated Audubon bird sanctuary and nice spot for a stop to enjoy the panoramic views of the Lake Worth Lagoon and to bird watch. Re-enter Palm Beach Island and, at the roundabout, head north (left) on A1A.

Jump forward to 1170 S. Ocean Blvd., the Bath and Tennis Club (see page 44) to continue with the key points of interest for your shortened tour.

CONTINUING WITH THE FULL-LENGTH PALM BEACH LOOP TOUR

To enjoy a more complete driving tour, continue south for a few miles on South Flagler Drive, with scenic views of the Lake Worth Lagoon and Intracoastal Waterway, until Summa Street, where you turn right (where South Flagler Drive veers away from the waterfront). Head west 2 blocks and turn left onto South Olive Avenue, also known as SR 5. Head south over the Palm Beach Canal into the city of Lake Worth, where the road changes names to North Federal Highway.

CITY OF LAKE WORTH, INCLUDING LAKE AVENUE

Heading south on North Federal Highway for a few miles, you will be driving through Lake Worth, a charming coastal community known for its relaxed vibe, featuring a quaint downtown shopping and dining district along Lake and Lucerne Avenues. When you reach Lake Avenue, turn left and drive a few blocks to cross the Lake Worth Bridge back to Palm Beach Island. If you have the time, though, you may want to stop for a stroll in downtown Lake Worth.

In addition to the unique shops, restaurants, and bars, a visit to the Cultural Council of Palm Beach County (palmbeachculture.com) in the landmarked

Robert M. Montgomery building at 601 Lake Ave. is recommended. The facility features a visitor center, art exhibits, and a gift shop that specializes in items made in the Palm Beaches.

The Cultural Council of Palm Beach County has been advocating for local arts for four decades.

The Lake Worth Casino Beach Complex is a great place to see the ocean.

LAKE WORTH CASINO BUILDING & BEACH COMPLEX
10 S. Ocean Blvd.

Driving over the Lake Worth Bridge, you will be looking directly at the Lake Worth Casino Building, which is part of an expansive public park and beach facility. Stop here for lunch or to see the ocean. Local noted architect Rick Gonzalez, American Institute of Architecture, led the 2013 restoration and expansion of the 1922 historic casino building, which now offers restaurants, shops, and an ice cream parlor, all overlooking the ocean. The most popular restaurant for lunch here is Benny's on the Beach, which is located directly on the pier. A walk out to the end of the pier is also recommended (there is a small entrance fee).

REENTERING PALM BEACH ISLAND & BILLIONAIRE'S ROW

Little Red Schoolhouse
2185 S. Ocean Blvd.

To continue your tour, drive north on A1A on Palm Beach Island, reentering the town of Palm Beach. You will pass through the Par 3 Golf Course (on both sides of the road) and by Phipps Ocean Park, where you can see the

The Little Red Schoolhouse was the first school in southeast Florida.

Little Red Schoolhouse, the first school in southeast Florida, dating to 1886. This building also doubled as the first church in South Florida from 1889 as Bethesda-by-the-Sea (an Episcopal church) until Bethesda II was built in 1894. As A1A turns right and curves toward the ocean at the so-called Sloan's Curve, you enter into the famed "Billionaire's Row." There are many famous residences (and residents) along this stretch. Please note that residences are private.

IL PALMETTO
1500 S. Ocean Blvd.

Commissioned by the immensely wealthy Philadelphia industrialist Joseph Widener in 1930, the 42-room, 68,000-square-foot "Il Palmetto" was built in the Italian Renaissance Palazzo style by Maurice Fatio, one of the most important architects in Palm Beach during the 1920s. The house is connected with the beach and pool cabana via a tunnel under A1A (as with many houses in Palm Beach), just before the road curves off the ocean at Widener's Curve.

CASA APAVA
1300 S. Ocean Blvd.

Built in 1919 for the Bolton political family of Ohio by architect Abram Garfield, the youngest son of President Garfield, the landmarked 26,000-square-foot Casa Apava was the most expensive house to ever sell in the United States in 2004, when it sold for $70 million, according to *Forbes* magazine.

THE BATH & TENNIS CLUB
1170 S. Ocean Blvd.

The Bath and Tennis Club (BTC) will be to your right as you pass the roundabout on your left. The exclusive private club was built in 1926 and was designed by architect Joseph Urban, an important architect for the last Austrian emperor, who later was considered to be the originator of American Art Deco.

MAR-A-LAGO
1100 S. Ocean Blvd.

After you drive to the right of the round a bout, just past the Bath and Tennis Club to continue north, Mar-a-Lago will be on your left. Built in 1927 by the acclaimed architects Marion Sims Wyeth and Joseph Urban for the heiress and grand dame socialite Marjorie Merriweather Post (Mrs. E.F. Hutton), Mar-a-Lago is a National Historic Landmark (one of only two in Palm Beach County). *Mar-a-Lago* is Spanish for "Sea-to-Lake," referring to the estate's 20 acres reaching from the ocean back to the lake. Six hundred workers labored for more than three

Mar-a-Lago is a National Historic Landmark, private club, and sprawling estate.

years to build this estate, using Italian stone, over 30,000 Spanish and Portugese tiles, marble floors, and 20,000 handmade red clay roof tiles from Cuba. Upon her death in 1973, Post willed the estate to the US government as a Winter White House for presidents and visiting foreign dignitaries. After realizing the immense cost of maintenance and the difficulty of maintaining security for diplomats, the government returned the estate to the Post Foundation, which listed it for sale for $20 million. The Post family did not maintain the property, expecting to sell it, but there was so little interest that the city approved its demolition to make way for smaller homes before it was declared a National Historic Landmark in 1980. Donald Trump finally acquired the historic estate in 1985 for $5 million, plus $3 million for the home's furnishings. Trump renovated the estate, adding a 20,000-square-foot ballroom to the 58 bedrooms and 33 bathrooms. Other notable furnishings are the 29-foot-long *pietra dura* marble top dining table, 12 fireplaces, and three bomb shelters. In the 1990s, Trump turned part of the estate into a private club. Many celebrities and notable personalities have been guests at Mar-a-Lago. For example, Michael Jackson and Lisa Marie Presley spent their honeymoon at the estate, staying in the tower bedroom. In 2012, Mar-a-Lago was voted the number-one historic building in the state of Florida by the Florida chapter of the American Institute of Architecture. Today, the 77,000-square-foot, 126-room mansion is dubbed the "Winter White House" of President Donald Trump, who resides with his family in a private section of the massive estate.

The Mar-a-Lago pool is seldom seen by the public.

President Trump in Palm Beach

Donald John Trump (born June 14, 1946) is the 45th and current president of the United States. As is widely known, prior to entering politics, he was a successful businessman and television personality. President Trump has had a dominant presence in and around Palm Beach since the early 1980s. Although his relations with the local community have not always gone smoothly, over time, Trump has garnered widespread respect and praise for his passion for Palm Beach and Mar-a-Lago, which he has been credited for saving and meticulously restoring. Since taking office in 2017, President Trump has used Mar-a-Lago as a Camp David–style presidential retreat, welcoming dignitaries and heads of state, such as the prime minister of Japan and the president of China, generating enormous attention for Palm Beach from national and international press.

CASA NANA
780 S. Ocean Blvd.

One of the finest examples by legendary Palm Beach architect Addison Mizner, this 30,000-square-foot estate was built in 1925 for Chicago tycoon George S. Rasmussen, founder of the National Tea Company who named the house after his wife. Later the estate was the residence of Mary Woolworth Donahue. The living room contains a 16th-century fireplace that King Henri II of France had made for his mistress, Diana De Poitiers. The fireplace's engraved double Ds refer to her; the H above stands for the king. In addition to the original circular stair tower leading to an oceanfront master suite, the estate has 9 bedrooms and 14 baths.

EL SOLANO
720 S. Ocean Blvd.

Built in 1919 by Addison Mizner for Harold Vanderbilt, the 14,000-square-foot estate El Solano has had many famous residents, including John Lennon and Yoko Ono.

Harold Vanderbilt, John Lennon, and Yoko Ono have all stayed in El Solano.

WORTH AVENUE

As you enter the center of the town of Palm Beach, you'll see the Clock Tower to the right marking the entrance to Worth Avenue (on your left). If you haven't visited yet, this might be a good opportunity to turn on to the avenue for a visit. See the section on Worth Avenue, on page 13.

Palm trees shade the charming sidewalks of Worth Avenue.

THE "400"
400 S. Ocean Blvd.

Designed in 1962 by prominent architect Edward Durrell Stone and widely known as Florida's first incorporated condominium, this sleek building is the most polished architectural example of Palm Beach Modernism and is reminiscent of Stone's work for the American Embassy in New Delhi, India, and the Kennedy Center in Washington, D.C.

VILLA DEL SARMIENTO
150 S. Ocean Blvd.

The 30,000-square-foot estate Villa del Sarmiento was built in 1924 by Addison Mizner for Philadelphia millionaire Anthony "Tony" Biddle and his wife, Mary Duke, the North Carolina tobacco heiress.

SOUTHWAYS
130 Barton Ave.

This 14,000-square-foot Beaux-Arts mansion was built in 1920 by the New York architectural firm Hoppin and Koen for Theodore Frelinghuysen, a member of New Jersey's greatest political dynasty. It became known as the "Winter White House" after President Warren Harding stayed there as a guest.

Southways has housed Theodore Frelinghuysen and President Warren Harding.

THE CHURCH OF BETHESDA-BY-THE-SEA
141 S. County Rd.

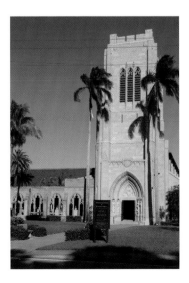

The congregation of Bethesda-by-the-Sea found their lasting home in their third and final church location. Notable church architect Ralph Adams Cram designed this Episcopal church in 1926. Tucked behind the church is the Cluett Memorial Garden, a peaceful hideaway.

The third and current Bethesda-by-the-Sea Episcopal Church was built in 1926.

Tropical flora surrounds the Breakers Palm Beach.

THE BREAKERS PALM BEACH

1 S. County Rd.

Inspired by the Medici Palace in Rome, the current building opened during the 1926–27 season and is listed on the National Register of Historic Places. See page 8 for more information.

PARAMOUNT BUILDING

139 N. County Rd.

The Palm Beach elite once paid $1,000 to reserve balcony box seats for a 13-week season here in the "Millionaire's Movie Theater." Box seat season tickets guaranteed great views of performers from top names of the day such as W.C. Fields, George Gershwin, Jack Benny, Danny Kaye, Ed Sullivan, Bob Hope, and Barbra Streisand. The Paramount is an office building today that still shows off architect Joseph Urban's unique style and skill.

ST. EDWARD ROMAN CATHOLIC CHURCH

142 N. County Rd.

St. Edward Roman Catholic Church was built in 1926 in the Spanish Renaissance style with an elaborate interior. St. Edward was the favorite church of many notable Palm Beach Catholic families. It was frequented by Kennedy family members, including President John F. Kennedy, for more than 60 years.

St. Edward Roman Catholic Church demonstrates Spanish Renaissance architecture.

LA QUERIDA

1095 N. Ocean Blvd.

Built by Addision Mizner in 1924 for department store tycoon Rodman Wanamaker, this 15,000-square-foot mansion became known as the "Kennedy Estate" when Joseph Kennedy Sr. purchased it in 1933. It later became known as the "Winter White House" for his son, President John F. Kennedy. The Kennedy family sold the home in 1995. See "President Kennedy in Palm Beach," page 30.

If time allows, continue your trip to the north end of the island where there is a roundabout. Heading back to the south, take the first right onto Indian Road, then left onto North Lake Way to return to the heart of Palm Beach.

"FORE AND AFT"

1221 N. Lake Way

Built in 1939 and designed by the acclaimed architect Belford Shoumate, this Art Deco house was named "the House of the Future" at the 1939 World's Fair in New York. In keeping with the nautical modernist theme, the house's name "Fore and Aft" references the commonly used terminology on a ship meaning "at the front and rear." Many famous personalities have lived in and visited this house, including First Lady Eleanore Roosevelt and former prime minister of Poland Ignacy Jan Paderewski.

CORAL CUT

As you continue to drive south on North Lake Way, the street runs parallel to the water with wonderful views of the Lake Worth Lagoon before making a sharp turn into Coral Cut. Landmarked by the town of Palm Beach,

Coral Cut is a pathway through exposed coral that makes up the geological base of the island. Photo courtesy of Michael Cushman.

Biltmore Condominium

the Coral Cut exposes the coral ridge geological base of Palm Beach Island. Make a right turn after you pass through Coral Cut, which leads you back to North Lake Way. Continue to head south.

"THE VICARAGE"
448 N. Lake Way

Built in 1897 as the home of the vicar of the Episcopal Church of Bethesda-by-the-Sea, this private residence has since had many famous residents. The architecture is reminiscent of the pre-Mediterranean Revival era in Palm Beach.

BILTMORE CONDOMINIUM
150 Bradley Place

North Lake Way turns into Bradley Place as you continue south. The Biltmore was originally built in 1926 and opened as the Spanish-themed Alba Hotel. The building became an exclusive condominium in 1981.

The nondenominational Royal Poinciana Chapel was built in 1898.

ROYAL POINCIANA PLAZA
340 Royal Poinciana Way

Continuing south crossing Royal Poinciana Way, you'll see an impressive 11-foot bronze statue of Henry Flagler to your left in the median to the east of the intersection. Just after the intersection on the right as you cross Royal Poinciana Way is the Royal Poinciana Plaza. Notable architect John Volk created the plaza in 1957. This Palm Beach landmark is one of the largest examples of commercial Regency architecture in the area. This was the site of the original Hotel Royal Poinciana built by Henry Flagler (see the historic marker along the path). Today, after a complete restoration and the addition of new boutiques and restaurants, the plaza is experiencing a major revival.

FLAGLER MUSEUM, WHITEHALL
One Whitehall Way

Continuing south on the same road (now called Cocoanut Row), you'll pass by Whitehall on the right (heading south). Henry Flagler's estate, built in 1902, is now a museum. See detailed information about the estate museum on page 4.

ROYAL POINCIANA CHAPEL

Directly next to Whitehall, the church was built in 1898 and was largely financed by Flagler, who insisted it be nondenominational (Christian) to serve the needs of his many hotel guests.

SOCIETY OF THE FOUR ARTS

2 Four Arts Plaza, Palm Beach, FL 33480; (561) 655-7227; fourarts.org

Take a break and enjoy the view at the Four Arts Botanical Gardens and Philip Hulitar Sculpture Garden. These outdoor spaces are just a piece of all the culture society has to offer. You'll find more information about the Society of the Four Arts on page 63.

Rick's Tips

For generations, visitors to Palm Beach have fantasized about what it would be like to visit one of the beautiful mansions, meet some of the famous residents, or even experience what it would be like to be a "Palm Beacher" for a day. Here's how visitors can do just that: Buy a ticket to a charity event!

Philanthropic activities for social and cultural causes are deep rooted in the social fabric of the Palm Beaches and also provide relatively easy access for visitors to get an inside glimpse of Palm Beach. Particularly during the Season, from December through April, there are multiple events every day, many of which can be attended by visitors. Prices for tickets range from as little as $40 for "Evening on Antique Row," which benefits the Historical Society of Palm Beach County, to $1,000 for a ticket to the legendary Red Cross Ball at Mar-a-Lago, where you can dance with the high society, prominent politicians, and royalty. You'll be sure to find one to fit your budget.

All these events, whether simple or glamorous, are typically "hosted" by a group of prominent Palm Beachers—you never know who you'll meet! Remember proper attire is a must. Calendar information about society events can be found at palmbeach dailynews.com/society /social-calendar/ and notables.palmbeachpost .com/calendar.

Charity events in Palm Beach include the American Red Cross Ball.

CHAPTER 2

MORE ON & OFF
THE ISLAND

Palm Beach County offers many cultural, sporting, and nature activities for visitors. The region boasts the "diversity without the density" of its metropolis neighbors to the south in Broward and Miami–Dade Counties. Based on the comments and feedback from thousands of guests and visitors the author has welcomed to the Palm Beaches, here is a short list of the most significant things to do.

Beaches

Palm Beach boasts 47 miles of coastline, so it makes sense that the most popular activity for visitors to Palm Beach is going to one of the many beautiful, pristine beaches. A German tourist once joked, "Only Palm Beach can afford to pour Perrier into the ocean to make the water so sparkly clear."

Indeed, due to the proximity of Palm Beach at the easternmost point on the Florida peninsula, protruding out into the warm waters of the turquoise blue Gulf Stream, average ocean temperatures range from 74°F in January to 85°F in August. The average day air temperatures range from 75°F in January to 90°F in July. There are all types of beaches available between Jupiter in the north to Boca Raton in the south: beaches in natural preservations, at county and state parks, beaches with activities and programming, and romantic secluded beaches. You can find a complete list of beaches on the Discover the Palm Beaches website (thepalmbeaches.com/beaches), but here is a recommended short list on Palm Beach Island to consider:

White sandy beaches are a highlight of Palm Beach.

PALM BEACH, MIDTOWN BEACH

Close by and easy to access, the Midtown Beach is a great beach to visit when combining other activities in Palm Beach, such as lunch or shopping. The beaches are well maintained with lifeguards and limited facilities (one bathroom and one shower). Public parking is available right along South Ocean Drive.

Midtown Beach

PALM BEACH ISLAND, NORTH END BEACHES

Ideal for beachgoers looking for a secluded, romantic beach visit, the beaches at the north end can only be reached via bicycle because there is no public parking. There are no facilities, so take something to drink with you. Take the Lake Trail north (see The Lake Trail, page 23), and you'll find that there are beach accesses at many of the east/west streets. In particular, the beaches at the east end of Reef Road, Mediterranean Road, Caribbean Road, Arabian Road, and Indian Road are particularly beautiful and secluded. Lock up your bike in the path near the road. There are no lifeguards at this beach. Please remember the adjacent residences are private property.

PHIPPS OCEAN PARK

2201 S. Ocean Blvd., Palm Beach, FL 33480

A 10-minute drive south, but still located within the town of Palm Beach, this expansive public beach features bathrooms, showers, shady picnic areas, and a nice, sparsely visited beach. You can also view the Little Red Schoolhouse here (see page 42). Lifeguards are on duty here. There is metered parking.

North end beach access points guide visitors over the dunes.

LAKE WORTH CASINO BUILDING & BEACH COMPLEX

10 S. Ocean Blvd., Lake Worth, FL 33460; lakeworth.org/visitors/
casino-building-and-beach-complex

A 15-minute drive south along A1A from the center of Palm Beach, this expansive public park is the area's best beach for families. It is also a great option for lunch or a late afternoon cocktail at Benny's on the Beach, which is located on the public pier. There are playgrounds, a public pool (restricted hours), and picnic tables. The historic casino building, recently refurbished and expanded, offers restaurants, shops, and an ice cream parlor, all overlooking the ocean. This beach, which has lifeguards, is also open at night, a rarity in Palm Beach County. This is also a convenient stop on a regional driving tour south to Boca Raton (see page 81), and a great destination in itself.

The Lake Worth Casino is a 15-minute drive south of Palm Beach.

Peanut Island

Peanut Island offers a wonderful beach-day experience, particularly on windy days when rough seas make it difficult to go swimming at other beaches directly on the ocean.

A small, man-made tropical island in the Lake Worth inlet close to the separation point between Singer and Palm Beach Islands, Peanut Island also houses a park for camping, fishing, snorkeling, and other recreational activities. Visitors and beachgoers at the 79-acre island can also visit the historic nuclear bunker built for former president John F. Kennedy during the Cold War. Walking tours are offered through the facility. The area around Peanut Island is a boaters' paradise, with many shallow areas and sandbars on which to anchor.

The island can be reached by water taxi from the Sailfish Marina or on a Peanut Island Ferry (200 E. 13th St., Riviera Beach, FL 33404; 561-844-7969; peanutislandferry.com) from the Riviera Beach Municipal Marina, which departs every 30 minutes.

Peanut Island is a small, man-made island in the Lake Worth inlet. Photo courtesy of Discover the Palm Beaches.

JOHN D. MACARTHUR BEACH STATE PARK

10900 Jack Nicklaus Dr., North Palm Beach, FL 33408; (561) 624-6952;
macarthurbeach.org

Also known as MacArthur Beach, this is undoubtedly one of the most beautiful
natural beaches in Palm Beach County and is the county's only state park.
Located on Singer Island, just to the north of Palm Beach Island, MacArthur
Beach offers natural trails, boardwalks, kayaking, picnic facilities, special
events, and, of course, 2 miles of pristine beaches. No lifeguards.

OCEAN REEF PARK

3860 N. Ocean Blvd.; Riviera Beach, FL 33404

Located on Singer Island, the island immediately to the north of Palm Beach
Island, Ocean Reef Park is a very nicely maintained county beach park that
is also popular for snorkeling or free diving. The beach is lifeguarded and
protected from passing boats. The reef is very close to the beach and can be
seen even at high tide, making it great for beginners who may be a little wary of
traveling too far out in the ocean. The park features a playground, picnic area,
ample free parking, and restrooms and showers onsite.

JUNO BEACH

14775 US 1; Juno Beach, FL 33408

Known as the area's best dog-friendly beach with miles of beach access, Juno
Beach is one of the most popular local beaches. There are separate areas for
fishing, swimming, and surfing, and this beach is great for families because it
has a large parking area right off the beach entrance, as well as restrooms and
picnic areas. The 990-foot pier is also very popular, and this beach also has the
added attraction that you can combine your beach experience with a visit to the
Loggerhead Marinelife Center (see page 107) to learn about the sea turtles that
nest along this beach.

DELRAY BEACH

Atlantic Avenue, Delray Beach, FL 33483

This beach has the advantage that beachgoers can combine their beach visit
with a stroll down the very popular Atlantic Avenue and enjoy the "Old Florida"
beach-town atmosphere of Delray Beach. There are shops and restaurants up
and down the avenue that are great for lunch or a tropical cocktail.

Arts, Culture & Entertainment

Identified by many publications as Florida's Cultural Capital, Palm Beach County is home to some of the oldest, most reputable cultural institutions in the state. The county was one of the first in Florida to support many of the local cultural institutions with bed tax dollars through the Cultural Council of Palm Beach County (palmbeachculture.com), which is also a great source of information about cultural happenings in the county. Here is a short list of the most notable cultural venues:

SOCIETY OF THE FOUR ARTS
2 Four Arts Plaza, Palm Beach, FL 33480; (561) 655-7227; fourarts.org

The Society of the Four Arts was founded in 1936 to offer quality cultural programming for the resort community of Palm Beach, focusing on drama, art, music, and literature. Today, "the Four Arts" offers a dynamic lineup of cultural programming, including notable speakers, concerts, films, educational programs, and art exhibitions. The expansive lakefront campus is home to

the elegant Philip Hulitar Sculpture Garden, the Gioconda and Joseph King Library, the Dixon Education Building, and the Four Arts Botanical Gardens, which is maintained by the Garden Club of Palm Beach. The gardens were designed in 1938 to help new residents in South Florida learn about gardening in the state's tropical climate. The Four Arts is a nonprofit charity, and all programs are open to the public. The Esther B. O'Keeffe Gallery Building, originally designed by Addison Mizner, is home to a gallery that features a diverse and ever-changing schedule of traveling art exhibitions. The building also includes

The Four Arts Plaza features unique sculptures.

a 700-seat auditorium with top-of-the-line sound and lighting for concerts, lectures, and films. The auditorium is home to the popular live broadcasts of Metropolitan Opera: Live in HD and National Theatre of London productions, offered fall through spring.

KRAVIS CENTER FOR THE PERFORMING ARTS
701 Okeechobee Blvd., West Palm Beach, FL 33401; (561) 832-7469; kravis.org

The Raymond F. Kravis Center for the Performing Arts is the most significant performing arts venue in the Palm Beaches and one of the premier performing arts centers in the Southeast. Highly visible at the entrance into downtown West Palm Beach at the "top of the hill" on Okeechobee Boulevard, the Kravis Center was the catalyst for downtown's renaissance in the 1990s. A diverse selection of performances are offered, including major Broadway shows, internationally renowned orchestras, famous recording artists, as well as classical ballet and modern dance presentations. The world-class Kravis Center opened fully funded in 1992 and today stands as a $100 million facility with a remarkable $82 million from private sources, individuals, and corporations and an additional $18 million from governmental sources.

The Kravis Center for the Performing Arts sits amid water and palm trees.

The Kravis Center includes four venues: the 2,195-seat Alexander W. Dreyfoos Jr. Concert Hall, the flexible 305-seat Marshall E. Rinker Sr. Playhouse, the 291-seat Helen K. Persson Hall, and the outdoor Michael and Andrew Gosman Amphitheatre, with a capacity for 1,400 patrons. More than 500,000 patrons attend some 800 events each year. Many regionally based arts organizations perform at the Kravis Center regularly, such as Miami City Ballet, Palm Beach Symphony, and the critically acclaimed Palm Beach Opera. During the 2016–17 25th anniversary season, the Kravis Center itself presented more than 400 performances featuring acclaimed artists from every discipline.

PALM BEACH OPERA

1800 S. Australian Ave., Ste. 301, West Palm Beach, FL 33409; (561) 833-7888; pbopera.org

Founded in 1961, the fully professional Palm Beach Opera offers a variety of cultural programs from December through April, including Opera @ The Waterfront, a free outdoor concert with Palm Beach Opera's orchestra and chorus at the Meyer Amphitheatre; fully staged mainstage opera productions at the Kravis Center for the Performing Arts; and a variety of community concerts for youth and adults. The main productions feature internationally acclaimed guest artists.

The Palm Beach Opera performs at the Kravis Center.

Pan's Garden at the Preservation Foundation of Palm Beach displays native plants and unique art. Photo courtesy of Preservation Foundation of Palm Beach

PALM BEACH DRAMAWORKS

201 Clematis St., West Palm Beach, FL 33401; (561) 514-4042;
palmbeachdramaworks.org

Located in the heart of lively downtown West Palm Beach on Clematis Street, this is one of the most highly respected professionally operated theater companies in Florida. The theater focuses on producing timeless, provocative, award-winning works, typically four plays during the Season and one or two musicals during the summer. A new experimental theater on the second floor showcases new and developing works. Palm Beach DramaWorks is a "must" for any theatergoer visiting the area.

THE ROYAL ROOM CABARET AT THE COLONY HOTEL PALM BEACH

155 Hammon Ave., Palm Beach, FL 33480; (561) 655-5430 or (561) 659-8100;
theroyalroom.com

Hailed as one of the top cabarets in the country, the Royal Room offers world-class cabaret-style performances by national and internationally recognized performers in an intimate dining room setting. With only a hundred seats, the room's setting allows you to not only experience great performances, but to feel every aspect of the artists' touch, as they captivate, charm, and delight. As a quintessential Palm Beach experience like no other, these shows are very popular, and reservations are highly recommended.

NORTON MUSEUM OF ART

1451 S. Olive Ave., West Palm Beach, FL 33401; (561) 832-5196; norton.org

The largest fine art museum in Florida, the Norton Museum of Art is one of the most important cultural mainstays in Palm Beach County. The museum was founded in 1941 by industrialist Ralph Hubbard Norton, who commissioned notable architect Marion Sims Wyeth to design and build the Art Deco/Neo-classical original structure. The original entrance faced South Olive Avenue and the Intracoastal Waterway. Today its collection includes over 7,000 works, with a concentration in European, American, and Chinese art as well as contemporary art and photography.

There are notable works from George Bellows, Georgia O'Keeffe, Jackson Pollock, Paul Manship, Peter Paul Rubens, Anthony van Dyck, Claude Monet, Paul Gauguin, Georges Braque, Marc Chagall, Henri Matisse, and Pablo Picasso. The museum is currently undergoing a monumental expansion, led by the internationally acclaimed Lord Norman Foster, expected to be completed by 2018. Art After Dark, Thursday, 5 to 9 p.m., offers tours and special activities. Admission is free during the expansion. Closed Mondays.

PRESERVATION FOUNDATION OF PALM BEACH

311 Peruvian Ave., Palm Beach, FL 33480; (561) 832-0731; palmbeachpreservation.org

After many historically significant buildings were destroyed in the area during the 1970s, a group of prominent citizens created the Preservation Foundation, a charitable foundation with the goal of preserving the architectural history and heritage of the town of Palm Beach. Since its creation, this private foundation has been instrumental in saving many important Palm Beach landmarks for future generations.

Today the foundation boasts extensive historical archives and offers a busy schedule of lectures, book signings, presentations, movie showings, and events throughout the Season (Dec through Apr), many of which are open to the public with a small entry fee. In addition, visitors can obtain a printed walking tour guide of Midtown Palm Beach, which highlights important buildings and landmarks in the vicinity, including Pan's Garden, the foundation's public garden featuring Florida native plants exclusively.

The Armory Art Center

For artistically inclined visitors or locals, a great way to enrich your experience of the Palm Beaches is by taking one of the many art classes offered at the historic Armory Art Center in West Palm Beach. The art school offers nearly 100 courses annually for artists of every age and level in 12 state-of-the-art studios. Courses are offered in ceramics, digital arts, drawing, glass fusing, jewelry, painting, printmaking, fibers, sculpture, and 20 exhibitions are hosted annually in 4 galleries. The Armory's Visiting Master Artist Workshop Series brings together participants and contemporary master artists from all over the country for unparalleled educational experiences. Now in its 18th year, the series caters to artists of all skill levels and diverse disciplines. You can combine a class with a stay at the charming Grandview Gardens Bed & Breakfast, which is located directly across the street.

For more information, contact the Armory Art Center, 811 Park Place, West Palm Beach, FL 33401; (561) 832-1776; armoryart.org.

OTHER NOTEWORTHY CULTURAL POINTS OF INTEREST IN THE REGION

MALTZ JUPITER THEATER

1001 E. Indiantown Rd., Jupiter, FL 33477; (561) 575-2223; jupitertheatre.org

Hailed as Florida's largest professional not-for-profit regional theater, this highly regarded company continues to draw regional and national attention with its award-winning musicals and plays that frequently garner plenty of Carbonell Awards, South Florida's equivalent of the Tony Awards.

ANN NORTON SCULPTURE GARDEN

2051 S. Flagler Dr., West Palm Beach, FL 33401; (561) 832-5328; ansg.org

Located in the El Cid Historic District of West Palm Beach, the former residence of sculptor Ann Weaver Norton (1905–1982), widow of Ralph Hubbard

Norton, was designed by architect Maurice Fatio and is listed in the National Register of Historic Places. The 1.7-acre property has expansive views of the Intracoastal Waterway and features many works of Mrs. Norton, as well as a collection of more than 250 species of tropical palms, cycads, and exotic plants. Be sure to visit the late artist's studio and view her impressive sculptures in the garden.

The Ann Norton Sculpture Garden displays grand Norton works.

BOCA RATON MUSEUM OF ART

501 Plaza Real, Boca Raton, FL 33432; (561) 392-2500; bocamuseum.org

Located in the heart of Boca Raton in Mizner Park, this fine-art museum boasts significant works of art from 18th-, 19th-, and 20th-century European and American masters, modern and contemporary works, and a major collection of West African tribal art and Oceanic art.

THE WICK THEATRE & COSTUME MUSEUM

7901 N. Federal Hwy., Boca Raton, FL 33487; thewick.org

This regional theater presents classic musicals and houses a museum for iconic Broadway costumes. Tours of the costumes should be reserved in advance.

West Palm Beach

When the immensely wealthy Henry Flagler, cofounder of Standard Oil, established Palm Beach as the first resort destination in the United States in 1894 with the opening of the Royal Poinciana Hotel, he also was instrumental in the incorporation of West Palm Beach, which became the first incorporated city in South Florida. The city was meant to provide infrastructure for his resort and to become a thriving, year-round community for a diverse population. Located directly across the three bridges from Palm Beach Island, the city of West Palm Beach is the county seat and largest city in Palm Beach County as well as the heart of the region's economic and cultural environment.

West Palm Beach sits across three bridges from Palm Beach Island.

A wonderful attribute of this city is the 5-mile waterfront along the Lake Worth Lagoon–Intracoastal Waterway with panoramic views of Palm Beach Island. As the oldest incorporated city in South Florida, Palm Beach boasts 16 historic districts (mostly residential), 9 of which are on the National Register of Historic Places. The historic districts are all located within a few blocks of the lagoon, mostly to the south and north of downtown. The most notable historic districts are El Cid, Prospect Park, Flamingo Park, Grandview Heights, Mango Promenade, and Old Northwood.

Downtown West Palm Beach is very walkable and offers abundant public parking. You can park your car in one of the parking garages and take one of the complimentary trolleys that stop at numerous key locations around downtown. Getting around by bike is also highly recommended.

The most important cultural attractions in West Palm Beach are the Norton Museum of Art, Kravis Center for the Performing Arts, and Palm Beach DramaWorks, which are all featured in the "Arts, Culture & Entertainment" section of this book (see pages 63–69). Otherwise, there are two main areas of interest to visit in downtown: The Clematis Street/Waterfront Park vicinity and CityPlace, a rejuvenated mixed-use area of downtown. This section highlights the most important points of interest in downtown and throughout the city.

Bike Sharing & Touring

One of the best ways to see West Palm Beach is on a bike. The waterfront offers a multipurpose path for cyclists and pedestrians along much of the 5-mile stretch, and downtown streets are generally wide enough to make bikers feel welcome. The city has an agreement with SkyBike to offer convenient and inexpensive bike-sharing services in and around downtown West Palm Beach with bike kiosks.

Unlike many other bike-sharing systems, SkyBikes are equipped with locks, so you can keep your bike with you as long as you want as you start and stop. Be aware that the "meter" keeps ticking until you return the bike to an official bike kiosk. The meter jumps to a reasonable 24-hour rate past a certain threshold. The mobile device app is free. For more information call (561) 412-1643 or visit skybikewpb.com.

WEST PALM BEACH VISITORS CENTER

(561) 881-9757, visitpalmbeach.com

Located directly on the downtown Waterfront Park at the east end of Clematis Street, the West Palm Beach Visitors Center provides extensive information about current events in the West Palm Beach area. In addition, visitors can book a guided bike tour, a sunset cruise (highly recommended), or make arrangements for other water sports activities and excursions such as paddleboarding and kayaking. Open seven days a week.

CLEMATIS STREET & WATERFRONT PARK

downtownwpb.com

The historic "main street" of West Palm Beach, Clematis Street, is at the heart of the West Palm Beach Arts & Entertainment District and offers a diverse selection of restaurants, bars, performing arts venues, and nightclubs. Although there are some boutiques, this area is primarily popular in the evening for entertainment. The east end of Clematis Street opens to Waterfront Park, where there are bandstands, public docks, and the West Palm Beach Visitors Center.

Every Thursday from 6 to 9 p.m., Clematis by Night offers free weekly concerts directly on Waterfront Park. This event draws thousands of people and features the area's best country, rock, R&B, reggae, blues, soul, swing, and Latin music. The West Palm Beach Greenmarket, one of the most popular farmer's markets in South Florida, takes place every Saturday on Waterfront Park from 9 a.m. to 1 p.m., October through May.

Art is never far on Clematis Street.

CITYPLACE
cityplace.com

CityPlace has really driven the economic revival of downtown. This lively, upscale, pedestrian- and family-friendly area with shops, restaurants, and entertainment is where you go to see a movie and possibly combine it with dinner. AMC CityPlace 20, the largest multiplex cinema complex in West Palm Beach, features 20 theaters, including an IMAX theater.

Although mostly corporate chain restaurants are to be found in CityPlace, the selection is diverse and the quality is generally good. Most notably, the Italian restaurant Il Bellagio, located on the charming main square, offers consistently good food and service with outside dining overlooking the main fountain. In addition to entertainment, CityPlace offers the best shopping in downtown.

THE PALM BEACH ZOO & CONSERVATION SOCIETY
1301 Summit Blvd., West Palm Beach, FL 33405; (561) 547-9453; palmbeachzoo.org

Originally a botanical garden, this highly acclaimed zoo houses some 700 animals from Florida; North, South, and Central America; Australia; and Madagascar. The diverse tropical vegetation makes this a nice outing for adults and children alike. Tucked away on the shore of beautiful Baker Lake in the heart of the zoo, the Tropics Café is a pleasant hideaway offering full-service dining in a unique air-conditioned facility complete with an Amazon Basin theme. Open seven days a week.

Shops, restaurants, and entertainment draw families to CityPlace.

SOUTH FLORIDA SCIENCE CENTER & AQUARIUM

4801 Dreher Trail N., West Palm Beach, FL 33405; (561) 832-1988; sfsciencecenter.org

A great excursion for families (ideal for a bad weather day). Highlights of this recently expanded and renovated facility include a dinosaur exhibit, 10,000-square-foot aquarium, and Palm Beach County's only public planetarium.

RICHARD & PAT JOHNSON PALM BEACH COUNTY HISTORY MUSEUM

300 N. Dixie Hwy., West Palm Beach, FL 33401; (561) 832-4164; historicalsocietypbc.org

Located inside the restored 1916 courthouse in downtown West Palm Beach and operated by the Historical Society of Palm Beach County, this county-wide museum brings alive the remarkable story of local history with a combination of permanent and traveling exhibits. There's also a nice gift shop with literature about local and Florida history.

The Palm Beach County History Museum displays local history. Photo courtesy of Discover the Palm Beaches.

RAPIDS WATER PARK

6566 N. Military Trail, Riviera Beach, FL 33407; (561) 848-6272; rapidswaterpark.com.

The largest water park in South Florida with 30 acres of attractions, among them 35 water slides (including dual 7-story speed slides) and a 0.25-mile lazy river. There are also slides for children and toddlers.

DIVA DUCK AMPHIBIOUS TOURS

600 S. Rosemary Ave., West Palm Beach, FL 33401; (561) 844-4188; divaduck.com

One of the most enjoyable ways to see some of the most important sites of West Palm Beach and Palm Beach for adults and children alike is by taking a tour with Diva Duck. The 75-minute, fully narrated tour is open air (but covered) over land and sea, taking participants through parts of historic West Palm Beach and Palm Beach. The amphibious vehicle, which sits up high for great views, starts with a land tour and then rides into the Intracoastal Waterway for a relaxing cruise to see some of Palm Beach's most beautiful mansions and yachts. Tours start at CityPlace in West Palm Beach and are regularly scheduled, with some variations for weather and special events on the waterfront.

LION COUNTRY SAFARI

2003 Lion Country Safari Rd., Loxahatchee, FL 33470; (561) 793-1094; lioncountrysafari.com

Originally developed by a group of South African and British entrepreneurs who wanted to bring the experience of an African game park to America, Lion Country Safari was the first drive-through safari park in the United States when it opened in 1967. The park, home to over 900 animals, still remains one of the most visited tourist attractions in Florida. Among the more notable species on display at the park are lions, white rhino, chimpanzees, zebras, and giraffes. Located about 12 miles west of West Palm Beach.

Lion Country Safari is home to more than 900 animals. Photo courtesy of Discover the Palm Beaches.

OTHER ATTRACTIONS & POINTS OF INTEREST IN THE AREA

PALM BEACH PHOTOGRAPHIC CENTRE

415 Clematis St., West Palm Beach, FL 33401; (561) 253-2600; workshop.org

Founded in 1985 as a nonprofit, PBPC offers a regular schedule of photography classes and workshops for all skill levels and a variety of interests. The 33,000-square-foot, state-of-the-art facility also features regular exhibits from local and award-winning photographers and is known for hosting the annual FOTOfusion every January, an international festival of photography and digital imaging. PBPC also features the Pro Shop for Photographers, supplying your needs for "all things photographic."

THE MANDEL PUBLIC LIBRARY OF WEST PALM BEACH

411 Clematis St., West Palm Beach, FL 33401; (561) 868-7700; wpb.org/departments/library

Located on bustling Clematis Street in the heart of downtown West Palm Beach, the largest library in the region loans out books and offers performances, classes, research, entertainment, technology, music, and more. Of particular interest for visitors are the 142 computers available for public use, including 50 on the 4th floor in the Grand Reading Room, which also has nice views across the city. Out-of-town visitors are encouraged to visit the library and take advantage of its services. A café offers refreshments.

MORIKAMI MUSEUM & JAPANESE GARDENS

4000 Morikami Park Rd., Delray Beach, FL 33446; morikami.org

Easily accessible from I-95, a visit to Morikami Gardens can be combined with a road trip to Boca Raton and/or the scenic drive along coastal A1A (see regional road trips). This highly regarded center for Japanese arts and culture boasts rotating exhibitions, tea ceremonies, festivals, and expansive Japanese gardens with strolling paths, a world-class bonsai collection, lakes teeming with koi, and other wildlife as well as a wider 200-acre park featuring nature trails, pine forests, and picnic areas. Add at least one or two hours to your agenda for this stop. For lunch, consider the open-air Cornell Café (nonmembers must pay museum admission to dine in the café).

YESTERYEAR VILLAGE AT THE SOUTH FLORIDA FAIRGROUNDS

9067 Southern Blvd., West Palm Beach, FL 33421; southfloridafair.com

Located on 10 acres inside the South Florida Fairgrounds, this quaint "town" is alive in Florida history; it's as though you've been transported to a different era and a simpler life. It's a re-created historic village with 20 historic structures,

Morikami Gardens is a center for Japanese art and culture. Photo courtesy of Discover the Palm Beaches

including a church, country store, and historical artifacts from 1895 through 1945. The Sally Bennett Big Band Hall of Fame Museum is also in the village, the only big band museum in the United States.

COMPASS COMMUNITY CENTER

201 N. Dixie Hwy., Lake Worth, FL 33460; (561) 533-9699; compassglcc.com

Located in charming downtown Lake Worth, Compass is one of the largest LGBTQ community centers in the Southeastern United States. Boasting a spacious, well-equipped, professionally managed community center offering a variety of services, social activities, and events throughout the year to the community, Compass is a great resource for LGBTQ residents and visitors alike in the Palm Beaches.

DR. MARTIN LUTHER KING JR. MEMORIAL PARK

2200 N. Flagler Dr., West Palm Beach, FL 33407

Located in Currie Park north of downtown West Palm Beach, this is one of the largest memorials commemorating the legacy of Dr. Martin Luther King Jr. The park, a testament to the many noteworthy historic and cultural contributions of the African American community in the Palm Beaches, contains numerous plaques and photos honoring Dr. King's life, family, and speeches as well as the civil rights movement. The highlights are a bronze sculpture of Dr. King backdropped by cascading water on a granite wall and the display of flags representing areas of great influence to King's life.

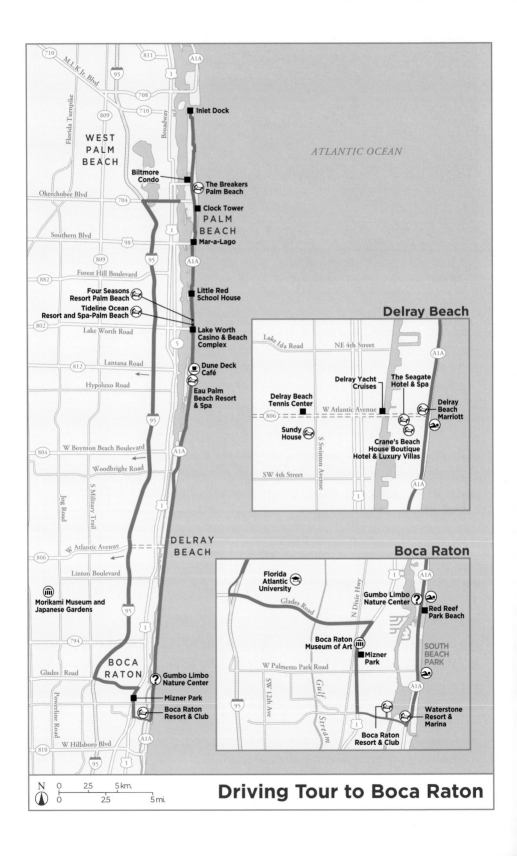

Driving Tour to Boca Raton

ATLANTIC OCEAN

WEST PALM BEACH

Inlet Dock

Biltmore Condo

The Breakers Palm Beach

Clock Tower

PALM BEACH

Mar-a-Lago

Little Red School House

Four Seasons Resort Palm Beach

Tideline Ocean Resort and Spa-Palm Beach

Lake Worth Casino & Beach Complex

Dune Deck Café

Eau Palm Beach Resort & Spa

Morikami Museum and Japanese Gardens

DELRAY BEACH

BOCA RATON

Gumbo Limbo Nature Center

Mizner Park

Boca Raton Resort & Club

Delray Beach

Lake Ida Road

NE 4th Street

Delray Beach Tennis Center

Delray Yacht Cruises

W Atlantic Avenue

The Seagate Hotel & Spa

Delray Beach Marriott

Sundy House

S Swinton Avenue

Crane's Beach House Boutique Hotel & Luxury Villas

SW 4th Street

Boca Raton

Florida Atlantic University

Glades Road

N Dixie Hwy

Gumbo Limbo Nature Center

Red Reef Park Beach

SOUTH BEACH PARK

Boca Raton Museum of Art

Mizner Park

W Palmetto Park Road

SW 12th Ave

Gulf Stream

Boca Raton Resort & Club

Waterstone Resort & Marina

N   0   2.5   5 km.
    0   2.5   5 mi.

CHAPTER 3

REGIONAL ROAD TRIPS

In addition to the town of Palm Beach and the immediate surroundings in neighboring West Palm Beach, the
region boasts a few noteworthy excursions to popular
destinations. One of the most popular excursions is an
extended drive south to Boca Raton with a drive back up
along the coast on A1A.

RICK'S TIPS As previously mentioned, one of the most popular excursions in the area is the drive along scenic A1A. My recommendation is to take your time and enjoy the ride along the mostly two-lane, winding road. The tour I've suggested for you in the book is less about the destination and more about the views along the route, ideal for a convertible or SUV. However, the points of interest I have included are noteworthy and, time allowing, you should plan your tour with a few stops along the way. For example, you might want to combine shopping and lunch at Mizner Park in Boca Raton or on Atlantic Avenue in Delray Beach with the drive back along the coast with no more stops. The views along A1A are best when driving from south to north, so you have the sun to your back and can better see over the tall hedges mostly to your left.

Driving Tour South to Boca Raton—Returning on A1A to Palm Beach

With no stops, the so-called "Palm Beach Grand Loop" tour would take about 90 minutes. Assuming you are beginning your tour in the town of Palm Beach, head west to I-95 and then drive south to Boca Raton, exiting at Glades Road (25 minutes), then head east to US 1, and then turn right. Head south, then turn left (east) on East Camino Real to access A1A. Head north on A1A along the coast to Palm Beach. You can significantly shorten this tour by taking the "Self-Guided Scenic Driving Tour" of Palm Beach as described on pages 35–56.

MIZNER PARK

327 Plaza Real, Boca Raton, FL 33432; miznerpark.com

Exiting I-95 at Glades Road, head east driving past Florida Atlantic University on your left. Turn right at US 1 to head south. Mizner Park will be on your left. One of the most popular points of interest for visitors to Boca Raton, this redeveloped mixed-use area of downtown boasts a fine selection of upscale shops and restaurants, theaters and department stores, and an outdoor amphitheater with regularly scheduled events and concerts. The Boca Pink

Minzer Park includes fine shops, restaurants and entertainment. Photo courtesy of Discover Palm Beaches.

Mediterranean Revival–style buildings and charming promenade along Plaza Real makes this a hip stop to have lunch, shop, and gain an impression of Boca Raton's upscale vibe.

BOCA RATON RESORT

501 E. Camino Real, Boca Raton, FL 33432; (561) 395-6766; bocaresort.com, bocahistory.org

Heading south on US 1, turn left on to East Camino Real. You will be entering the original resort area designed by Addison Mizner. Heading east, you will see the Boca Raton Resort on your left. Built in 1926 as the Ritz Carlton Cloister Inn, this sprawling, iconic resort is famous for its Boca Pink and Mediterranean Revival architecture. Your stop here can be as short as a drive-by in the front for photos or you may want to take a historic walking tour, which is offered on the second and fourth Tuesday of January of the month, through early May, at 2 p.m. by the Boca Raton Historical Society.

The 1½-hour strolling tour reveals the hotel's story—its hoteliers, architecture, historic turning points (such as the World War II years), and its incredible role in Boca Raton's history since the 1920s. The Boca Raton Resort is private and only hotel guests or club members may enter the resort, so the tour is a great option to see this landmarked hotel. *Note:* RSVP is required and must be confirmed by 11 a.m. on tour date. Call the Boca Raton History Museum for reservations.

Boca Raton

Boca Raton is the southernmost city in Palm Beach County and was incorporated in 1924. The name comes from Spanish *Boca de Ratones* and is roughly translated to mean "a shallow inlet of sharp-pointed rocks which scrape a ship's cables." Residents of the city have kept the pronunciation of Boca Raton similar to its Spanish origins. In particular, the "Raton" in "Boca Raton" is pronounced with a long "o," not a short "o," which is a common mispronunciation by those not native to the region. The city today is known for gated communities, golf courses, private clubs, and its Boca Pink Mediterranean Revival theme, initially inspired by the great Florida architect Addison Mizner, who influenced the city's early development. Boca Raton has a strict development code for the size and types of commercial buildings, building signs, and advertisements that may be erected within the city limits. No outdoor car dealerships are allowed in the municipality. Additionally, no billboards are permitted.

GUMBO LIMBO NATURE CENTER

1801 N. Ocean Blvd. (A1A), Boca Raton, FL 33432; gumbolimbo.org

Continue east on East Camino Real and turn left (north) on A1A; the nature center will be on your left after a short drive. This slice of authentic Florida nature is named after Florida's native gumbo limbo tree (*Bursera simaruba*). Explore the boardwalk nature trail through the hardwood hammock. Visit the outdoor marine aquariums and the sea turtle rehabilitation center. During certain times of the year, the center leads evening turtle walks on the beach, where visitors can observe sea turtles laying their eggs (reservations required). This is a popular stop for children in particular. Plan 30 to 60 minutes for this stop. See Gumbo Limbo Nature Center in the Waterways & Coastal Natural Areas section, page 108.

DELRAY BEACH—ATLANTIC AVENUE

downtowndelraybeach.com

Continue your drive north on A1A to Atlantic Avenue. As one of the most charming seaside towns in South Florida, Delray Beach at Atlantic Avenue is a highly recommended stop. This is a great location to have lunch or a coffee before taking a stroll down the avenue to see some of the sites. Turning on to Atlantic Avenue from A1A, drive west over the Intracoastal Waterway and find parking along the street or follow signs to public parking, which is either free or inexpensive all around town. See Delray Beach, page 62, for details on visiting the beach itself.

Atlantic Avenue is a vibrant main street with restaurants, shops, bars, sidewalk cafés, and galleries. There is waterfront dining on the Intracoastal Waterway. There are festivals and events along the avenue throughout the year, including major professional tennis tournaments at the Delray Beach Tennis Center, also located on Atlantic Avenue. You can either choose to drive from one end to the other on Atlantic Avenue or stop here for one to two hours (or all afternoon).

PALM BEACH ISLAND

When you are back on A1A and driving north, you will pass through smaller coastal towns until you reach the Boynton Inlet, which is where you enter the southern tip of the famous Palm Beach Island at Manalapan. Almost immediately upon entering the island, you notice the lush tropical canopy shading the road—you are driving through the middle of one of the largest estates on Palm Beach Island, known as Gemini (2000 S. Ocean Blvd., Manalapan), which encompasses both sides of the road. The 33-bedroom, 72,000-square-foot estate was built for the late William B. Ziff, a publishing magnate.

A little farther north, at 1100 South Ocean, still in Manalapan, you will pass the 34,000-square-foot estate Eastover, built by high-society architect Maurice Fatio for Harold Vanderbilt, and listed on the National Register of Historic Places.

DUNE DECK CAFÉ
100 N. Ocean Blvd., Lantana, FL 33462; dunedeckcafe.com

If you haven't made a stop until now on your tour, take a break at this charming, casual restaurant situated in the dunes of Lantana Public Beach with a spectacular view of the ocean. Great for breakfast or lunch.

LAKE WORTH CASINO BUILDING & BEACH COMPLEX
10 S. Ocean Blvd., Lake Worth, FL 33460

Situated a 10-minute drive farther north on Palm Beach Island, the Lake Worth Casino Beach Complex is the family beach of the area. Children and adults can

swim safely with lifeguards on duty. The recently refurbished historic casino building also offers restaurants, shops, and an ice cream parlor, all overlooking the ocean. Enjoy lunch at Benny's or a walk to the end of the pier for a small entrance fee.

Restaurants, shops, and an ice cream parlor overlook the ocean at the Lake Worth Casino Beach Complex.

Reentering the Town of Palm Beach & Billionaire's Row
The return trip to Palm Beach from this regional road trip goes by Billionaire's Row and a collection of notable Palm Beach landmarks. Notice the first school built in southeast Florida (Little Red Schoolhouse, page 42). The retreats and "Winter White Houses" of two presidents are well worth a look. See Mar-a-Lago, page 44. Stop to browse, shop, eat, or watch the glamorous people on Worth Avenue. See Worth Avenue, page 13. Other major landmarks include: Church of Bethesda-by-the-Sea, the Breakers, Royal Poinciana Chapel, Flagler Museum, and the Society of the Four Arts. To continue the drive up the coast on the Palm Beach Loop Self-Guided Scenic Tour, go to page 42.

Driving Tour to the North on A1A to the Jupiter Inlet

 Located approximately 20 miles to the north of Palm Beach Island, another popular excursion within Palm Beach County is a leisurely drive up the coast to the Jupiter Inlet, one of the most picturesque spots in South Florida. In 2008, the area was designated by congress as the Jupiter Inlet Lighthouse Outstanding Natural Area.

The excursion can be made earlier in the day and combined with a visit to area beaches or the lighthouse or in the late afternoon or early evening to be combined with some of the most romantic waterfront dining in South Florida. With no stops, the drive to Jupiter takes about 25 minutes.

From West Palm Beach, drive north on US 1, turn right on Blue Heron Boulevard in Riviera Beach and follow A1A over to Singer Island. Continue heading north to where A1A merges back with US 1. Continue north, and as you enter Juno Beach, veer to the right back onto A1A, which leads to the beaches. Continue north until you intersect with US 1 again, which is just before the inlet. You can return to Palm Beach on I-95 (quickest) or stay on US 1 to head south again.

JOHN D. MACARTHUR BEACH STATE PARK
10900 Jack Nicklaus Dr., North Palm Beach, FL 33408; (561) 624-6952; macarthurbeach.org

MacArthur Beach is the only state park and one of the most beautiful natural beaches in Palm Beach County. The park features natural trails around Singer Island, kayaking, special events, and picnic sites along with 2 miles of ocean beach.

LOGGERHEAD MARINELIFE CENTER
14200 US. 1, Juno Beach, FL 33408; (561) 627-8280; marinelife.org

The Loggerhead Marinelife Center at Juno Beach promotes ocean conservation. There are numerous exhibits, annual events, and programs, including the very popular Evening Turtle Walks from June 1 to July 31 and the Evening Hatchling Release Walks in August (must register online). Read more about the Loggerhead Marinelife Center in the Waterways & Coastal Natural Areas section, page 107.

THE JUNO BEACH PIER
14775 US 1 Juno Beach, FL 33408

The 990-foot pier offers a welcome opportunity to stop and stretch your legs and take a look at the ocean (the pier opens 30 minutes before sunrise). The

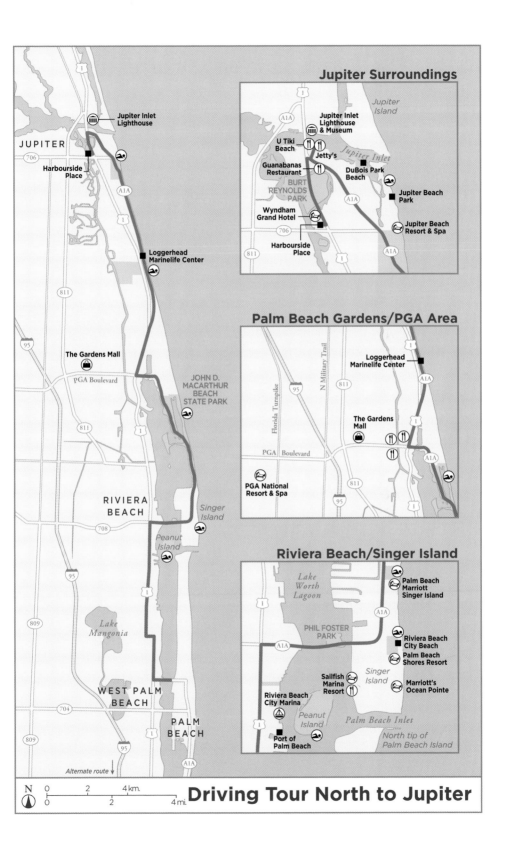

Driving Tour North to Jupiter

Jupiter Surroundings

Jupiter Island

Jupiter Inlet Lighthouse & Museum

U Tiki Beach

Jetty's

Jupiter Inlet

Guanabanas Restaurant

DuBois Park Beach

BURT REYNOLDS PARK

Jupiter Beach Park

Wyndham Grand Hotel

Jupiter Beach Resort & Spa

Harbourside Place

JUPITER

Jupiter Inlet Lighthouse

Harbourside Place

Loggerhead Marinelife Center

Palm Beach Gardens/PGA Area

Loggerhead Marinelife Center

Florida Turnpike

N Military Trail

The Gardens Mall

PGA Boulevard

PGA National Resort & Spa

The Gardens Mall

JOHN D. MACARTHUR BEACH STATE PARK

Riviera Beach/Singer Island

RIVIERA BEACH

Singer Island

Peanut Island

Lake Worth Lagoon

Palm Beach Marriott Singer Island

PHIL FOSTER PARK

Riviera Beach City Beach

Palm Beach Shores Resort

Sailfish Marina Resort

Singer Island

Marriott's Ocean Pointe

Riviera Beach City Marina

Peanut Island

Palm Beach Inlet

Port of Palm Beach

North tip of Palm Beach Island

WEST PALM BEACH

PALM BEACH

Lake Mangonia

Alternate route ↓

N

0   2   4 km.

0   2   4 mi.

full-service Pier House features a friendly guest services team and snack bar, as well as a variety of fishing tackle, including rental poles and bait.

The Juno Beach Pier offers a perfect ocean view. Photo courtesy of the Loggerhead Marinelife Center.

The City of Jupiter

Jupiter is the northernmost city in Palm Beach County. The city is known for its natural beauty with upscale waterfront communities and public venues around the Jupiter Inlet, which is a natural inlet to the Atlantic Ocean. The area where the town now sits was originally named for the Hobe Indian tribe that lived around the mouth of the Loxahatchee River and whose name is also preserved in the name of nearby Hobe Sound. A mapmaker misunderstood the Spanish spelling "Jobe" of the Indian name "Hobe" and recorded it as "Jove." Subsequent mapmakers further misunderstood this to be the Latin translation of the god Jupiter, and they anglicized the name from Jove to "Jupiter."

JUPITER INLET LIGHTHOUSE & MUSEUM

500 Captain Armour's Way, Jupiter, FL 33469; (561) 747-8380; jupiterlighthouse.org

Built in 1860 and listed on the National Register of Historic Places, the Jupiter Inlet Lighthouse is located at the junction of the Indian and Loxahatchee Rivers. The Jupiter Inlet Lighthouse and Museum offers climbing tours to the top of the 103-foot lighthouse and a waterfront history museum in a restored World War II navy building known as "Station J," which was instrumental in identifying and destroying 30 German U-boats near the Florida coast during the conflict.

Indoor exhibits tell diverse stories of over 5,000 years of human habitation in and around the Jupiter Inlet and Loxahatchee River. Stroll along the brick walkways to discover the restored 1892 Tindall Pioneer Homestead exhibit, the 100-year-old Pennock Plantation Bell, and native plants and habitats.

Built in 1860, the Jupiter Inlet Lighthouse is the oldest man-made structure in Palm Beach County.

HARBOURSIDE PLACE

200 N. US 1, Jupiter, FL 33477; harboursideplace.com

Nestled along Jupiter's Intracoastal Waterway, Harbourside Place is an upscale mixed-use development featuring restaurants, shops, the Wyndham Grand Jupiter Hotel, and an outdoor amphitheater with free, regularly scheduled live entertainment.

Rick's Tips

For a late afternoon or early evening excursion to Jupiter, a visit to one of these restaurants is highly recommended:

U TIKI BEACH

1095 N. H A1A, Jupiter, FL 33477; (561) 406-2210; utikibeach.com

Caribbean food and drinks in a casual, island setting with deck and beach seating and spectacular water views toward the lighthouse. U Tiki does not accept reservations, so plan accordingly and try to arrive about an hour before sunset. The grounds are perfect for walking with a cocktail while waiting for a table.

JETTY'S WATERFRONT RESTAURANT

1075 N. H A1A, Jupiter, FL 33477; (561) 743-8166; jettysjupiter.com

Jetty's Waterfront Restaurant is a very popular, upscale, family-friendly restaurant with views of the lighthouse and a menu of just-caught seafood. No reservations are accepted, but you can get a cocktail and walk along the water while you wait.

GUANABANAS RESTAURANT

960 N. H A1A, Jupiter, FL 33477; (561) 747-8878; guanabanas.com

An institution in Palm Beach County and identified by many as one of the most romantic restaurants in Florida, Guanabanas is entirely open-air. You'll dine in a spectacular jungle-like setting directly on the water with woven tiki huts and coquina walkways that pass through lush tropical gardens. The restaurant specializes in seafood exclusively from Florida waters and also features live music from regionally and nationally recognized performers. Reservations are not accepted, but the wait for a table can be enjoyed by sipping a cocktail down by the water in one of the many lounge chairs. Get here an hour before sunset.

Harbourside Place features restaurants, entertainment, shopping, and lodging. Photo courtesy of Discover the Palm Beaches.

U Tiki offers tropical fare with a great view.

CHAPTER 4

A SPORTING PARADISE

With 160 golf courses, world-class tennis facilities, the National Croquet Center, deep-sea fishing opportunities, and a multitude of water-sports venues, the Palm Beach area has long been identified as a sporting paradise. Here are some top attractions.

Golf

Palm Beach has been designated Florida's golf capital, and it offers a wide range of options for the golfer. Visitors can play on Florida's oldest 18-hole course, the Breakers Old Course, or watch the best golfers in the world come for the PGA Tour's Honda Classic at the PGA National Resort and Spa. The Palm Beaches area is packed with award-winning championship golf courses and 40 public courses (and about 160 total in the county!).

You can find extensive information about where to play, where to take lessons, where to watch tournaments, or read about special deals by visiting Discover the Palm Beaches website (thepalmbeaches.com/golf). Here is a short list for you to consider.

PGA NATIONAL RESORT & SPA

400 Ave. of the Champions, Palm Beach Gardens, FL 33418; (561) 627-1804; pgaresort.com/golf/pga-national-golf

With five championship courses played by some of golf's greatest, this resort is considered the best in the area. Although the courses are officially only open to resort members and guests, visitors can often obtain tee times when calling ahead, in particular out of peak season (winter/spring). The courses include the Champion, redesigned by Jack Nicklaus; the Fazio and the Squire, designed by George and Tom Fazio; the Palmer designed by Arnold Palmer; and the Estate, designed by Karl Litten.

THE BREAKERS OCEAN COURSE

One S. County Rd., Palm Beach, FL; (561) 655-6611; thebreakers.com/golf

Originally designed by Alexander H. Findlay in 1896, this is Florida's oldest 18-hole course. Although private for club members and hotel guests, visitors can obtain tee times in off periods. The private course, which covers nearly 85 acres of the the Breakers' property, was redesigned in 2000 by famed golf course architect Brian Silva.

PALM BEACH PAR 3 GOLF COURSE

2345 S. Ocean Blvd., Palm Beach, FL 33480; (561) 547-0598; golfontheocean.com

Hailed as "one of the best par 3s you can play anywhere" by *Golf Digest* magazine, this popular public course was recently redesigned by Dick Wilson and Raymond Floyd. Nestled between the Atlantic Ocean and Florida's beautiful

Palm Beach golf courses offer ocean views.

Intracoastal Waterway, it features spectacular views of the ocean. Al Fresco restaurant, in the clubhouse, also offers breathtaking views and is highly recommended for breakfast, lunch, or dinner.

MADISON GREEN COUNTRY CLUB

2001 Crestwood Blvd. N., West Palm Beach, FL 33411; (561) 784-5225; madisongreengolf.com

With a 4.9 rating from *Golf Digest*, the Madison Green Country Club is considered one of the top Zagat-rated golf courses in South Florida. This par 72 golf course winds its way through nature preserves surrounded by pine barrens, hundreds of palm trees, oaks, and Florida native plants. Nature is abundant with native birds such as the great blue heron, sandhill crane, snowy egret, and various hawks calling the course their home. Although the address says West Palm Beach, this course is located in Royal Palm Beach, west of town.

Tennis

Palm Beach County is home to more than 60 private and public tennis centers, including tennis programs and facilities at most of the major resort hotels, such as the Boca Raton Resort & Club, Four Seasons Resort Palm Beach, The Breakers, PGA National Resort and Spa, and the Eau Palm Beach Resort & Spa.

Also a tennis haven, the 8,200-seat Delray Beach Tennis Center is an Association of Tennis Professionals (ATP) award-winning public facility located in downtown Delray Beach. The center hosts the Delray Beach Open every February, when the world's top professional tennis players "hit" the destination for the ATP World Tour and ATP Champions Tour competitions. Palm Beach County is also home to the Evert Tennis Academy in Boca Raton, which provides year-long intensive training to tennis enthusiasts and week-long courses geared toward visitors. Here is a short list of local public tennis facilities, which are available to visitors:

SEAVIEW PARK & PHIPPS OCEAN PARK TENNIS CENTERS (PALM BEACH ISLAND)

Seaview Park and Phipps Ocean Park Tennis Centers offer programs, drop-in play, lessons, clinics, mixers, tournaments, special events, and league play for children and adults throughout the year.

SEAVIEW PARK TENNIS CENTER

340 Seaview Ave., Palm Beach, FL 33480; (561) 838-5404

Seaview Park features 7 lit courts with shaded shelters and a practice wall and hosts a variety of adult and junior tournaments, parent-child round robins, evening doubles round robins, and league play. Instruction is available through private lessons and adult and junior clinics. The pro shop offers apparel, accessories, and racket stringing.

PHIPPS OCEAN PARK TENNIS CENTER

2201 S. Ocean Blvd., Palm Beach, FL 33480; (561) 227-6450; townofpalmbeach.com

The Phipps Ocean Park Tennis Center offers 6 tennis courts.

The Delray Beach International Tennis Championships draw a crowd. Photo courtesy of Discover the Palm Beaches

HOWARD PARK TENNIS CENTER

901 Lake Ave., West Palm Beach, FL 33401; (561) 833-7100

One of the oldest tennis centers in Palm Beach County, the well-maintained Howard Park Tennis Center is located immediately adjacent to downtown West Palm Beach in Howard Park. It offers 9 courts; 7 are lighted.

SOUTH OLIVE TENNIS CENTER

345 E. Summa St., West Palm Beach, FL 33405; (561) 635-5005

One of the most active tennis facilities in the area, South Olive Tennis Center offers 9 lighted courts.

Croquet

THE NATIONAL CROQUET CENTER

700 Florida Mango Rd., West Palm Beach, FL 33406; (561) 478-2300;
croquetnational.com

The National Croquet Center is the largest dedicated croquet facility in the world and has set a new standard for the sport of croquet. Built on 10 acres in West Palm Beach by the Croquet Foundation of America, the National Croquet Center features a 19,000-square-foot clubhouse that sits in the midst of a vast and near-perfect lawn where guests can choose to organize golf croquet lawn parties, basic instruction, and tournament competition.

Visitors are welcome and can participate in free "golf croquet" lessons offered every Saturday morning at 10 a.m. Reservations are required. Otherwise, experienced players can play for a daily rate of $30, including all equipment.

Fishing

Florida is often hailed as the Fishing Capital of the World, and the Palm Beaches play a big role in that title. From deep-sea fishing to freshwater fishing, the Palm Beaches are popular with anglers of all ages and levels of experience.

SALTWATER/DEEP-SEA FISHING

Located at the easternmost point on the Florida peninsula with the Gulf Stream just off shore, the coast off of Palm Beach Island has been popular for deep-sea fishing for generations. Visitors can find local private charters and drift boat fishing services at or near both the Riviera Beach Marina and the Sailfish Marina on Singer Island. Catches consist of kingfish, snapper, grouper, mahi-mahi, sailfish, cobia, barracuda, sharks, false albacore, and wahoo. Here is a short list of local services offered:

BLUE HERON FISHING

389 E. Blue Heron Blvd. (under the Blue Heron Bridge), Riviera Beach, FL 33404; (561) 844-3573; blueheronfishing.com

One of the largest and established drift boat fishing operations in the area, Blue Heron Fishing offers crews who have years of experience for family outings.

Fishermen enjoy the Juno Beach Pier. Photo courtesy of Discover the Palm Beaches.

Two half-day excursions depart daily. No reservations are necessary. The fare includes rod, reel, bait, tackle, and fishing license. If you've never gone fishing and you want to try it, drift boat fishing is a great way to start!

RIGHT HOOK FISHING CHARTERS
200 E. 13th St., Riviera Beach, FL 33404; (561) 452-4040; righthookcharters.net
Located at the Riviera Beach Marina, Right Hook Charters offers both drift boat fishing for smaller groups as well as private charters.

PRIVATE BOAT CHARTERS
There are numerous private charter operations in the area, in particular at the Riviera Beach City Marina (200 E. 13th St., Riviera Beach, FL 33404;

561-842-7806; rivierabeachmarina.com) and the Sailfish Marina (98 Lake Dr., Palm Beach Shores, FL 33404; 561-844-1724; sailfishmarina.com) on Singer Island (which has the largest concentration of charter boats available). The Sailfish Marina is also an attraction in itself with popular waterfront dining. For a complete listing of current private charter boats available, visit either of the marinas and/or their websites.

FRESHWATER FISHING

Lake Okeechobee in western Palm Beach County is the crown jewel of bass fishing in Florida. At 730 square miles, not only is it the largest freshwater lake in the state, but the second largest contained entirely within the lower 48 states. Lake Okeechobee is a favorite location for some of the biggest bass fishing tournaments in the world, like the Bassmaster Elite Series and FLW Tour. Catching bass over 8 pounds and five-fish bags over 30 pounds are common, especially during the spawning period in late winter. Sightseers and anglers can best access Lake Okeechobee from Torry Island next to the city of Belle Glade at the southeast corner of the lake (about 45 miles west of Palm Beach).

SLIMS FISH CAMP

215 Marina Dr., South Bay, FL 33493; (561) 996-3844; slimsfishcamp.com

Slims, on Torry Island, is one of the oldest continuously operating Okeechobee guide services on the lake, offering fishing trips for trophy bass, bluegill, and crappie (speck) with fully equipped bass boats, stocked with the recommended rods and reels. Four-hour to full-day excursions are offered.

Major Sports & Recreation Events

 Palm Beach County is home to some of the most significant sports and recreation events in the country. The impact of these major sporting events spills over into the cultural and social scene of Palm Beach during the peak months of December through April. In addition to multiple major golf and tennis events taking place throughout Palm Beach County, Wellington (located about 10 miles west of Palm Beach) is the equestrian capital of the world during the winter and spring months.

WINTER EQUESTRIAN FESTIVAL
3400 Equestrian Club Dr., Wellington, FL 33414; pbiec.coth.com

Taking place over 12 weeks every year from January to April as the largest show of its kind in the United States, visitors can see the finest horses and riders as they compete at the Palm Beach International Equestrian Center in Wellington in both show jumping and hunting. This is an equestrian festival like no other, featuring the best riders of their class—Olympians, adult amateurs, juniors, and children.

A major highlight for visitors is the weekly Saturday Night Lights Grand Prix Show, taking place every Saturday evening January through March, featuring food, live music, and the highest level of competitive show jumping in the country. Festivities typically begin at 6 p.m. and are free, except for parking. There are also galleries for shopping, wine and coffee bars, outdoor cafés, and a children's area.

GLOBAL DRESSAGE FESTIVAL
13500 S. Shore Blvd., Wellington, FL 33414; (561) 793-5867; gdf.coth.com

Another event that takes place at the Palm Beach International Equestrian Center, the Global Dressage Festival is the largest dressage circuit in the world with the concentration of Concours Dressage International (CDI) shows in Wellington. Top-echelon dressage riders travel from all over the world during the winter months to ride in these prestigious shows. The most popular night for visitors is the Friday Night Stars Grand Prix Dressage Freestyle event, which features the highest level of dressage competition as well as food and entertainment. Spectators will watch dressage combinations "dance" to music choreographed especially for them and their horse. Spectators hear everything from classic orchestral pieces to the latest Top 40 pop hits.

Horse Show 101

Attending a horse show can feel like stepping into a whole new world. Here are a few basic facts that might be helpful to make your equestrian experience more enjoyable:

- There are three main divisions at a hunter/jumper horse show: hunter, jumper, and equitation. In all three, a rider guides a horse over a set course of obstacles in a ring. However, each is scored differently. The jumper discipline is scored based on the objective speed and accuracy the rider has over the course. Hunter and equitation are based on a subjective judge of form over the course, with hunter classes focusing on the form of the horse and equitation classes focusing on the form of the rider. The main professional events in show jumping, such as the Olympics or Grand Prix events held at WEF's Saturday Night Lights events in Wellington, are the jumper discipline.

- Gender: Mare/Stallion/Gelding: A mare refers to an adult female horse. A stallion refers to an adult male horse still intact for breeding. Male horses that have been castrated are referred to as geldings and are the more common of the two male horses in the hunter/jumper world due to their milder temperaments.

- Age: Hunter/jumper horses are generally first shown at about 5 years of age until they are in their late teens to about 20 years of age. "Green" horses are younger and less experienced.

- Gait: A gait is the pattern of leg movement and pace in which a horse travels. The four gaits, from slowest to fastest, are walk, trot, canter, and gallop. Jumping events are done at the canter, occasionally speeding up to the gallop when riders are attempting fast times in a jump-off. The length of the average horse's stride at a canter is 12 feet.

- Tack: The gear associated with the horse, including all items it "wears" in order to be ridden.

- Dressage is the oldest equestrian discipline, dating back to the Renaissance and having its foundation in classical Greek horsemanship. The sport was developed to prepare war horses for battle. *Dressage* is French and roughly translates to "training." The object of dressage is the development of the physical ability of the horse, resulting in a calm and flexible animal that is confident and in perfect harmony with his rider. The objective of dressage is to have the horse perform under saddle with the degree of athleticism and grace that it naturally shows when free. As a result, dressage horses are shown in minimal tack.

- Horse shows at Palm Beach International Equestrian Center are casual outdoor events. Comfortable walking shoes are recommended so you can explore the entirety of the show grounds.

PALM BEACH INTERNATIONAL POLO SEASON

3667 120th Ave. S., Wellington, FL 33414; (561) 204-5687; internationalpoloclub.com

The International Polo Club Palm Beach is considered by many to be the premier polo destination in the world, hosting the largest field of high-goal teams and the most prestigious polo tournaments in the United States. The Palm Beach Polo Season runs from January through April and concludes with the celebrated U.S. Open Polo Championship final. Attracting celebrities and polo enthusiasts from around the world, the open welcomes everybody with a wide range of hospitality and guest seating such as grandstand viewing, field tailgating, and field-side champagne brunch at the Pavilion. Ticket prices for Sunday polo start at only $30 for stadium seating.

Gillian Johnston competes at the International Polo Club. Photo courtesy of Phelps Media Group

Competitive tennis is a major attraction in Palm Beach.
Photo courtesy of Discover the Palm Beaches

DELRAY BEACH OPEN

201 W. Atlantic Ave., Delray Beach, FL 33444; (561) 330-6000;
yellowtennisball.com

The world's only ATP Champions Tour Event and ATP World Tour Event, which takes place every February at the Delray Beach Stadium & Tennis Center, allow visitors to watch top-ranked players compete in these highly competitive, internationally televised tournaments. In addition to the tournaments, there are special events and parties along the iconic Atlantic Avenue district of Delray Beach.

THE HONDA CLASSIC

400 Ave. of the Champions, Palm Beach Gardens, FL 33418; thehondaclassic.com

This major, internationally televised PGA Tour tournament brings together many of the world's top golfers each February and March to compete for a $6 million purse at the PGA National Resort & Spa. Check the website for parking instructions.

THE PALM BEACHES MARATHON

From medal-holding veterans to local schoolchildren, people of all walks of life run this marathon, which takes place during the first half of December each year. The route is scenic with long stretches along waterways and the ocean, including the West Palm Beach waterfront on Flagler Drive. Family-friendly, race-related events take place all weekend. Visit palmbeachesmarathon.com for more information.

Crowds gather for a more intimate baseball experience, watching MLB teams train for the season at Roger Dean Stadium. Photo courtesy of Discover the Palm Beaches.

MAJOR LEAGUE BASEBALL SPRING TRAINING

The Palm Beaches boast two major league spring training facilities where baseball fans can watch four different teams practice and play against each other. In addition, visitors here in the summer can watch minor class A teams with the Florida State League, such as the Jupiter Hammerheads and the Palm Beach Cardinals.

The 6,800-seat Roger Dean Stadium (4751 Main St., Jupiter, FL 33458; 561-775-1818; rogerdeanstadium.com) in Jupiter is the spring training home of the St. Louis Cardinals and the Miami Marlins. The 6,400-seat Ballpark of the Palm Beaches (5398 Haverhill Rd., West Palm Beach, FL 33407; ballpark-palmbeaches.com) is the training facility for the Washington Nationals and Houston Astros. Other MLB teams from around the country visit for training games throughout the spring.

CHAPTER 5

NATURE & OUTDOOR ACTIVITIES

As one of the largest counties east of the Mississippi River, encompassing a large portion of Lake Okeechobee and the northeast Everglades, Palm Beach County is a paradise for outdoor and nature enthusiasts. Hiking, cross-country biking, bird-watching, horseback riding, canoeing, kayaking, paddleboarding, and recreational boating are abundantly available throughout the county. The sparsely populated interior western wetlands, including the northeast Everglades area, are ideal for visitors wanting to experience Florida's natural subtropical beauty and observe wildlife. The coastal region, well known for its beautiful beaches, also offers nature enthusiasts opportunities to experience coastal natural habitats and marine life.

Waterways & Coastal Natural Areas

Palm Beach County features 47 miles of Atlantic coastline as well as the parallel Intracoastal Waterway, which also runs through the wider 22-mile-long Lake Worth Lagoon, which separates the mainland from the barrier islands (including Palm Beach Island). Although much of the coastline has been developed, nature lovers and outdoor enthusiasts have plenty of options to get out and experience wilder areas along or near the beaches and waterways.

The Palm Beach coast boasts one of the highest concentrations of sea turtle nesting grounds in the world. Generations of locals and visitors alike have been captivated by these giant gentle sea creatures as they crawl onto the beach and lay their eggs under the star-filled night sky. Visitors also have opportunities to

The Palm Beach coast is vast. Photo courtesy of John D. MacArthur Beach State Park

see other marine life such as manatees, porpoises, stingrays, sharks, flying fish, and other exotic animals associated with the tropics.

All beaches are public lands, so anybody can walk on the beach. However, public access to the beaches is largely limited to public parks and easements as well as hotels and resorts. For information regarding beaches, go to pages 58–62. This section focuses on viewing and experiencing nature as well as other recreational activities along the coast.

JOHN D. MACARTHUR BEACH STATE PARK
10900 Jack Nicklaus Dr., North Palm Beach, FL 33408; (561) 624-6952; macarthurbeach.org

This state park on Singer Island boasts 2 miles of pristine beaches (without lifeguards) as well as natural trails, kayaking, special events, and more. Located just north of Palm Beach Island, MacArthur Beach is on the way north on A1A to Jupiter Inlet (see page 84).

Manatee sightings are common (more often in the winter), and the beach is widely known as a nesting ground for rare sea turtles, including the endangered loggerhead, the endangered green sea turtle, and, occasionally, the exceedingly rare leatherback. In addition, many interesting species of birds also visit the park, including the peregrine falcon, wood stork, and least tern.

Other amenities include the Nature & Welcome Center and Beach Outfitters Gift Shop, kayak rentals, a children's playground, nature trails, and picnic facilities. Special events are planned throughout the year, including moonlight concerts and the very popular sea turtle talk and walk events.

LOGGERHEAD MARINELIFE CENTER
14200 US 1, Juno Beach, FL 33408; (561) 627-8280; marinelife.org

Promoting conservation of ocean ecosystems with a special focus on threatened and endangered sea turtles, the Loggerhead Marinelife Center is located at Juno Beach. It is recognized as one of the most active nesting beaches for sea turtles in the world. Fun for the entire family, the expansive campus on the ocean includes a state-of-the-art, full-service veterinary hospital (one of a kind in South Florida) and a variety of exhibits, live sea turtles, and other coastal creatures.

Exhibits include a massive prehistoric Archelon sea turtle replica, saltwater aquaria, and displays of local wildlife, as well as educational displays about South Florida's marine environment. There are numerous annual events and programs, including the very popular Evening Turtle Walks from June 1 to July 31 and the Evening Hatchling Release Walks in Aug each year (must register online).

The Loggerhead Marinelife Center focuses on threatened and endangered sea turtles. Photo courtesy of Greg Lovett and Loggerhead Marinelife Center

GUMBO LIMBO NATURE CENTER

1801 N. Ocean Blvd. (A1A), Boca Raton, FL 33432

Named after Florida's native gumbo limbo tree (*Bursera simaruba*), this center offers visitors the chance to experience authentic Florida nature up close in a 20-acre nature preserve. Picnic tables are also available. Explore the boardwalk nature trail through the hardwood hammock. Visit the outdoor marine aquariums and the sea turtle rehabilitation center. During certain times of the year, the center leads evening turtle walks on the beach where visitors can observe sea turtles laying their eggs (reservations are required).

MANATEE LAGOON—FPL ECO-DISCOVERY

6000 N. Flagler Dr., West Palm Beach, FL 33407; (561) 626-2833; visitmanateelagoon.com

The 16,000-square-foot center features engaging, hands-on exhibits for visitors to learn all about these endangered and unique creatures as well as the natural wonders of the surrounding Lake Worth Lagoon. On cold winter days, the facility's observation deck is the ideal spot to view manatee herds basking in the warm-water outflows from Florida Power & Light Company's adjacent Riviera Beach Next Generation Clean Energy Center. Free admission and parking. Amenities include two levels of exhibit and observation areas, gift shop, café, and picnic facilities. Open Tuesday through Sunday, closed on holidays.

BOATING & RECOMMENDED BOAT TOURS

One of the most exciting ways to explore the waterways around Palm Beach is by renting your own boat! Or if you don't feel comfortable piloting a boat, then hire a captain or go on a boat tour. Boats and/or captains are available for hire at the Riviera Beach Marina and Sailfish Marina. Below is a short list of boats for hire and area boat tours:

BLUE WATER BOAT & JET SKI RENTALS

200 E. 13th St., Riviera Beach, FL 33404; (561) 840-7470; bluewaterboatrental.com

Located at the Riviera Beach Marina Village with boat and Jet Ski rentals. Great location to explore Peanut Island and the Intracoastal Waterway in your own boat.

ADVENTURE WATERSPORTS

98 Lake Dr., Palm Beach Shores, FL 33404; (773) 333-7723; adventurews.com

Offering private boat charters, with captain, for cruising the Intracoastal Waterway and the ocean. Snorkeling, swimming, wakeboarding, and tubing also possible.

Manatees in the lagoon. Photo courtesy of Discover the Palm Beaches

VISIT PALM BEACH

On the waterfront at N. Clematis St. & Flagler Dr., West Palm Beach, FL 33401; (561) 881-9757; visitpalmbeach.com

Evening sunset cruises, catamaran snorkeling excursions, kayak rentals, Jet Skis, paddleboards, and more.

MAJESTIC PRINCESS CRUISES

200 E. 13th St., Riviera Beach, FL 33404; (561) 899-4555; majesticprincesscruises.com

Offering regularly scheduled, themed, and event cruises out of the Riviera Beach Marina.

THE MANATEE QUEEN

1065 N. Ocean Blvd. (A1A), Jupiter, FL 33477; (561) 744-2191; manateequeen.com

Offering regularly scheduled midday and sunset cruises around the Jupiter Inlet, Loxahatchee River and Jupiter Island.

JONATHAN DICKINSON STATE PARK BOAT TOURS

16450 S.E. Federal Hwy., Hobe Sound, FL 33455; (561) 746-1466; jdstatepark.com /boat-tours

One of the most exciting boat tours in South Florida, these trips meander up the Loxahatchee River, one of Florida's federally designated Wild and Scenic Rivers, aboard the *Loxahatchee Queen III*. Often seen are alligators and the West Indian manatee as well as various types of bird and animal life, such as bald eagles, osprey, great and little blue herons, egrets, raccoons, Florida peninsula cooter turtles, and a variety of other species.

The Hakuna Matata catamaran shows visitors the best of Palm Beach from the water. Photo courtesy of Visit Palm Beach

Florida Everglades and Interior Wetlands

Visitors to Palm Beach can drive to the Everglades, Florida's "River of Grass," within 30 minutes from anywhere in Palm Beach County. In addition to Everglades National Park (nps.gov/ever), located about 90 minutes by car to the southwest of West Palm Beach, visitors in Palm Beach County can easily access other notable nature preserves much closer at the Arthur R. Marshall Loxahatchee National Wildlife Refuge (loxahatcheefriends.com) and within the Northeast Everglades Natural Area.

Here you will find numerous parks and nature preserves for hiking, biking, horseback riding, canoeing, and kayaking. Two of the most popular nearby parks easily accessible from the coast are Grassy Water Everglades Preserves and Riverbend Park.

GRASSY WATERS EVERGLADES PRESERVES
8264 Northlake Blvd., West Palm Beach, FL 33412; (561) 804-4985; wpb.org/grassywaters

Grassy Waters is a 23-square-mile wetlands ecosystem that serves as the freshwater supply for the City of West Palm Beach and the towns of South Palm Beach and Palm Beach Island. As one of the largest untouched, pristine areas of the northeast Everglades, this is a great spot for visitors who want to get

Grassy Waters is a preserved portion of the Everglades. Photo courtesy of Discover the Palm Beaches

a glimpse of the Florida Everglades without venturing too far from the coast. Visitors will see alligators, the endangered snail kite, bald eagles, great blue herons, and more. There are numerous hiking possibilities as well as naturalist-guided canoe and kayak trips. The mile-long Cypress Boardwalk is a pleasant stroll, and you're almost sure to see an alligator or two.

RIVERBEND PARK

9060 Indiantown Rd., Jupiter, FL 33478; pbcgov.com/parks/riverbend, loxahatchee river.org

Riverbend Park, located a few miles west of Jupiter on Indiantown Road, offers 10 miles of hiking, cycling, riding, and 8 miles of canoeing and kayaking on or around the federally designated Wild and Scenic Loxahatchee River, one of only two such designated rivers in Florida.

Visitors can rent cross-country bikes, canoes, and kayaks at Canoe Outfitters of Florida (561-746-7053, canoeoutfittersofflorida.com) near the park entrance.

Many people (including the author) consider a canoe trip down the Loxahatchee to be one of the most exciting nature excursions in South Florida, providing visitors with an adventurous, close-up look at Florida's nature, comparable to anything in the Everglades. Visitors commonly spot alligators, snakes, turtles, deer, bald eagles, bobcats, egrets, herons, otters, and more.

Limestone Creek Natural Area offers an escape into nature. Photo courtesy of Discover the Palm Beaches

Loxahatchee River is a slice of wilderness to explore by water.
Photo courtesy of Michael Ridgdill

Rick's Tips for Hiking

Most of the parks listed in this guide feature hiking trails, most notably Riverbend Park. However, there are many more nature preserves and wildlife management areas with great hiking, deep in Florida's natural habitats. Here are two of my favorites.

APOXEE WILDERNESS TRAIL

This trail in the first urban wilderness area in Palm Beach County offers a walk over and through the water supply of West Palm Beach. It's a fascinating 4.7-mile day hike featuring a mix of boardwalks, crushed limestone, and natural surfaces underfoot on a loop that includes a section of the Owahee Trail, a lengthy berm that runs through all of Grassy Waters Preserve (see page 111). Plenty of wildlife can be seen, including alligators. Directions: Head west on Okeechobee Boulevard in West Palm Beach for 4.6 miles until you get to Jog Road. Turn right onto Jog and look for the park entrance on your left near 3125 North Jog Road.

J.W. CORBETT WILDLIFE MANAGEMENT AREA

Sandwiched between the metropolises along the coast and the farmlands in the west, this 60,000-acre wildlife management area is an important refuge for native wildlife and a recreational paradise for outdoor lovers. You can explore pine flatwoods, cypress swamps, and a hardwood hammock on the Hungryland Boardwalk and Trail, which is well removed from hunting zones and is open year-round. There are also much longer hikes available, including the famous Florida Ocean to Lake Trail. Abundant wildlife can be seen. Directions: Travel 13 miles west of I-95 on Northlake Boulevard until the road ends at Seminole Pratt Whitney Road, then turn right and the park entrance will be on your left 3 miles north.

EVERGLADES AIRBOAT TOURS

For many visitors, a trip to the Florida Everglades is not complete without an exciting airboat ride. Driven by a caged airplane propeller mounted above the rear, these shallow draft boats are capable of traveling at relatively high speeds through the swamps. There are numerous airboat operations in South Florida. Following are the most highly rated operations in Palm Beach County.

Loxahatchee Everglades Airboat Tours & Rides
15490 Loxahatchee Rd.
Pompano Beach, FL 33321
(561) 901-0661
evergladesairboattours.com

West Palm Beach Airboat Rides
(561) 252-4030
westpalmbeachairboatrides.com

Airboats are driven by caged airplane propellers that get very loud. Photo courtesy of Discover the Palm Beaches

Kayaks give explorers a quiet chance to see South Florida waterways.

Canoeing, Kayaking & Paddle Boarding

 With numerous waterways, lakes, rivers, and wetlands, the Palm Beach area has numerous opportunities for canoeing and kayaking as highlighted in other chapters in this guide. For the avid canoe and kayak enthusiasts, below is a short list of the most popular locations from which to rent equipment and explore some of South Florida's most beautiful waters and wetlands.

VISIT PALM BEACH

On the waterfront at N. Clematis St. and Flagler Dr., West Palm Beach, FL 33401; (561) 881-9757; visitpalmbeach.com

Kayak rentals, Jet Skis, paddleboards, catamaran cruises, snorkeling tours, and rentals.

RIVIERA BEACH MARINA VILLAGE

190 E. 13th St., Riviera Beach, FL 33404; (561) 844-8408; rivierabeachmarina.com

Kayak rentals, dinner cruises, charter boats, dive boats, paddleboard rentals, and eco tours through Paddle Boarding Palm Beach.

SINGER ISLAND OUTDOOR CENTER

900 E. Blue Heron Blvd., Riviera Beach, FL 33404; (561) 839-5130; singerislandoutdoorcenter.com

Located at Phil Foster Park at the base of the Blue Heron Bridge. Offers kayaking, paddleboarding, and snorkeling gear.

RIVERBEND PARK / CANOE OUTFITTERS OF FLORIDA

9060 Indiantown Rd., Jupiter, FL 33478; (561) 746-7053; canoeoutfittersofflorida.com

Visitors can rent cross-country bikes, canoes, and kayaks near the park entrance. (See page 112 for more information on this park.)

ARTHUR R. MARSHALL LOXAHATCHEE WILDLIFE REFUGE

10216 Lee Rd., Boynton Beach, FL 33473; (561) 734-8303; loxahatcheefriends.com

Hiking and biking also available.

BLUELINE SURF & PADDLE COMPANY

997 N. A1A, Jupiter, FL 33477; (561) 744-7474; bluelinesurf.com

Kayaks, paddleboards, and surfboards with access to the Loxahatchee River

Biking

 As highlighted earlier in the guide, biking is one of the most popular activities in the Palm Beach area. A flat terrain makes it perfect for cyclists of all ages and levels of fitness. The area is particularly famous for the multipurpose paths along the Intracoastal Waterway in both Palm Beach and West Palm Beach.

PALM BEACH LAKE TRAIL ON PALM BEACH ISLAND

Once the main artery of transportation on Palm Beach, the Lake Trail today serves as a multipurpose path to explore the island. Bicycles have replaced the three-wheeled wicker rickshaws that carried visitors around the island from the 1890s through the late 1950s. The Lake Trail passes notable landmarks like the oldest house on the island and the former Kennedy family retreat. You can jump on or off anywhere on the path, which mainly runs along the Lake Worth Lagoon.

The longest section of the trail extends from Royal Poinciana Way to the northern tip of the island. The shorter but more historic section is between Royal Poinciana Way and Royal Palm Way. Many visitors start their tour by renting a bike at Palm Beach Bicycle Trail Shop (50 Cocoanut Row, palmbeachbicycle.com) on the south side of the Royal Poinciana Plaza, where parking is available. The staff offers helpful tips and can usually supply a map.

Starting the tour from the bike shop, enter the Lake Trail right at the Royal Poinciana Plaza, which at that location runs parallel to Cocoanut Row. For a detailed description of this tour, see page 23.

WEST PALM BEACH TRAILS

As mentioned earlier in the guide under West Palm Beach, one of the best ways to see this city is on a bike. The 5-mile waterfront of West Palm Beach offers a multipurpose path for cyclists and pedestrians from Currie Park on the north side of downtown all the way to Summa Street in the south end of the city. The city has an agreement with SkyBike (561-412-1643, skybikewpb.com) to offer convenient and inexpensive bike-sharing services in and around downtown West Palm Beach with bike kiosks.

Unlike many other bike-sharing systems, SkyBikes are equipped with locks, so you can keep your bike with you as long as you want as you start and stop. Be aware that the "meter" keeps ticking until you return the bike to an official bike kiosk. At some point, the meter jumps to a 24-hour rate, which is reasonable. The mobile device app is free.

Bicycles are the time-tested favorite mode of transportation around Palm Beach Island.

RIVERBEND PARK

9060 Indiantown Rd., Jupiter, FL 33478; pbcgov.com/parks/riverbend, loxahatcheeriver.org

Cyclists can enjoy 10 miles of paths along the federally designated Wild and Scenic Loxahatchee River. Cross-country bikes are available for rent at Canoe Outfitters of Florida (561-746-7053, canoeoutfittersofflorida.com). This park offers one of the few opportunities to do cross-country biking in South Florida nature. Visitors commonly spot alligators, snakes, turtles, deer, bald eagles, bobcats, egrets, herons, otters, and more.

Scuba divers get up close to ocean life. Photo courtesy of Discover the Palm Beaches

Scuba Diving & Snorkeling

 While visitors might think of the Florida Keys when considering scuba diving or snorkeling in Florida, the coast along Palm Beach is widely recognized among divers as the best diving area around the Florida Peninsula. There are numerous reefs in 40- to 80-foot depth, and due to the close proximity of the Gulf Stream right off shore, there is an incredible abundance of marine life. For example, Palm Beach is home to five of the seven species of sea turtles found throughout the world.

Over 300 species of fish life and several thousand species of coral, sponge, and other invertebrate life can be found just off shore, including goliath grouper, schools of spadefish, snappers, grunts, rays, green and spotted moray eels, spiny lobsters, and nurse sharks. In addition to the natural reefs, there are numerous shipwrecks and artificial reefs.

Other than a shore dive at Phil Foster Park (off Blue Heron Bridge, where you can also snorkel), all of the diving around Palm Beach is drift diving. There are numerous operators at the Riviera Beach Marina, Lake Park Marina, and Singer Island (mostly around the Sailfish Marina). Here is a short list of established operators:

DIVING

Narcosis Dive Charters
200 E. 13th St.
Riviera Beach, FL 33404
(561) 630-0606
narcosisdivecharters.com

Force-E Scuba Center
155 Blue Heron Blvd.
Riviera Beach, FL 33404
(561) 845-2333
force-e.com

Paradise Below Diving & Charters
200 E 13th St.
Riviera Beach, FL 33404
(855) 968-3483
paradisebelowdiving.com

Pura Vida Divers
2513 Beach Ct.
Riviera Beach, FL 33404
(561) 840-8750
puravidadivers.com

SNORKELING

Keylypso of the Palm Beaches
105 Lake Shore Dr.
Lake Park, FL 33403
(561) 718-2723
keylypso.com

Singer Island Outdoor Center
900 Blue Heron Blvd.
Riviera Beach, FL 33404
(561) 839-5130
singerislandoutdoorcenter.com

CHAPTER 6

SHOPPING & SPAS

The Palm Beach area offers the widest variety imaginable for shoppers. After going to the beach and playing golf, shopping is one of the favorite pastimes of visitors to the Palm Beaches. From exclusive boutiques on world-famous Worth Avenue at the top of the budget spectrum to the Palm Beach Outlets next to I-95, there is something for everybody in the Palm Beaches.

In addition to well-known department stores and retail outlets, the Palm Beach area is internationally recognized as a significant trading center for antiques, art, and luxury goods. For a complete overview of shopping in Palm Beach County, go to thepalmbeaches.com /shopping. This chapter features a short list of the top shopping areas.

Worth Avenue, Palm Beach

worth-avenue.com

Worth Avenue is the home of Palm Beach style and one of the most exclusive boutique shopping districts in the world. Worth Avenue's historical significance is detailed on page 13 in this guide. The avenue's romantic vias and celebrated boutiques offer the best of both resort and designer fashion, accessories, gifts, art, antiques, fine and casual dining, and home furnishings in a captivating atmosphere rich with Old World charm and historical glamour.

Worth Avenue is a charming mixed-use district of approximately 200 shops, boutiques, department stores, galleries, and restaurants as well as residences and offices. The major luxury brands are typically situated directly on the

Worth Avenue is a fashion mecca.

avenue. On the eastern end, Nieman Marcus and Saks Fifth Avenue are the largest anchor department stores.

Make sure to explore the so-called vias, the nine pedestrian passageways connected to the avenue on the south and north sides. Many of the most interesting, unique, non-corporate/chain retailers are located in the vias. Most shops close between 5 and 6 p.m. Monday through Saturday. Very few shops are open on Sunday. Shoppers can park for up to 2 hours for free directly on the avenue, but expect an expensive fine if you stay too long.

There is also valet parking at the Esplanade on the left shortly after entering Worth Avenue at the east end as well as at the Apollo lot on Hibiscus Avenue just off Worth, which is in the middle of the avenue. Metered parking is also available on Peruvian Avenue (1 block to the north of Worth Avenue).

Town Square, South County Road, Royal Poinciana Way & Sunset Avenue — Palm Beach

gscrapb.org, palmbeachchamber.com

In addition to Worth Avenue, Palm Beach has a few other noteworthy shopping areas with charming boutiques along South County Road between Seaview and Worth Avenues as well as around Royal Poinciana Way and Sunset Avenue. In addition to boasting some of the island's finest restaurants, these shopping districts are well known for consignment and second-hand shops.

For example, the Church Mouse (374 S. County Rd., Town Square) is recognized as one of the top donation-based resale shops in the country, operating for nearly 50 years and offering discounts up to 90 percent off original prices for designer labels such as Ferragamo, Jimmy Choo, Ralph Lauren, Brooks Brothers, Michael Kors, and more. Men and women's clothing, accessories, furniture, crystal, china, and books are available. Net proceeds go to charity.

Bookworms will also enjoy the Classic Book Shop (310 S. County Rd.) and the Palm Beach Book Store (215 Royal Poinciana Way). Both shops offer a wide variety, including fiction, nonfiction, biography, history, business, gift books, coffee table books, cookbooks, greeting cards, magazines, and newspapers (also international).

Downtown West Palm Beach

 If you are looking for a more urban, vibrant atmosphere, downtown West Palm Beach might be a good choice, especially if you would like to combine shopping with dining, going to the movies, or other entertainment. The two main areas of interest are CityPlace and the Clematis Street area (including neighboring streets).

CityPlace (cityplace.com) is a lively, upscale, pedestrian-friendly area with a mix of 80 shops, restaurants, movie theaters, sidewalk cafés, bars, and entertainment venues.

The Clematis Street area and the rest of downtown (downtownwpb.org) offer a diverse selection of retail and is recognized for its thriving art scene with numerous art galleries and regularly scheduled art exhibits and events. Much of the work of innovative artists can still be seen in the form of colossal murals and installations on buildings and parks throughout the downtown area.

Parking in downtown West Palm Beach is a piece of cake with public parking garages or lots on just about every other block. Downtown residents have joked that downtown West Palm Beach has more public parking spaces per resident than any other city in the United States. While that statistic has not been proven, visitors seldom have to walk more than a block from their parking space to most destinations throughout the city. In addition, there is inexpensive on-street metered parking, which is free after 7 p.m. (except at CityPlace).

After you have parked, moving around downtown is very easy with the free trolley system, which has stops at CityPlace, Clematis Street, and throughout downtown. You can hop on and off at any stop.

Check out the websites for complete business directories and event calendars.

PALM BEACH OUTLETS, WEST PALM BEACH
1751 Palm Beach Lakes Blvd., West Palm Beach, FL 33401; (561) 515-4400;
palmbeachoutlets.com

The newest shopping mecca in South Florida for bargain hunters, this is a mega retail destination featuring major outlet stores including Saks Off 5th and Nordstrom Rack. Whole Foods is also part of the action.

Other Major Shopping Malls in the Region

THE GARDENS MALL

3101 PGA Blvd., Palm Beach Gardens, FL 33410; (561) 622-2115;
thegardensmall.com

Arguably the nicest, upscale enclosed shopping mall in South Florida, the
2-story mall features 160 specialty shops and restaurants as well as Macy's,
Sears, Bloomingdale's, Nordstrom, and Saks Fifth Avenue.

MIZNER PARK

327 Plaza Real, Boca Raton, FL 33432; (561) 362-0606; miznerpark.com

After Worth Avenue in Palm Beach, Mizner Park is in the heart of downtown
Boca Raton. This outdoor shopping venue features specialty shops, theaters,
restaurants, and a Lord & Taylor anchor.

Antiques & Unique Boutiques

 With a high concentration of historic estates, neighborhoods, and
districts and a long tradition of high-end interior design, the Palm
Beach area has long been known as a treasure trove of antiques,
consignment shops, secondhand stores, and charming boutiques.
Designers and collectors from all over the world travel here to buy and sell
merchandise during the numerous art and antiques fairs. In addition to the more
upscale establishments along South County Road, Royal Poinciana Way, and
Sunset Avenue in Palm Beach mentioned above, those listed below are the most
commonly known areas with antiques, consignment, and secondhand shops.

SOUTH DIXIE, ANTIQUE ROW & GEORGIA AVENUE

Heralded by the *New York Times*, *Art & Antiques*, *Conde Nast Traveler*, and
Architectural Digest as one of the East Coast's premier antiques shopping districts, this area is one of Florida's most significant antiques design centers. There
are shops scattered along South Dixie in West Palm Beach starting just south
of Okeechobee Boulevard all the way into the city of Lake Worth. However,
the core of this district is the official West Palm Beach Antique Row Art &
Design District along South Dixie Highway between Belvedere and Southern
Boulevard.

In this charming district with more than 40 antiques shops, shoppers will find an impressive selection of 17th- to 20th-century antiques, fine and decorative arts, period deco, vintage, and modern furnishings, all within walking distance. A detailed list of current shops and restaurants can be found at westpalmbeachantiques.com.

Nearby and running parallel to South Dixie (but starting south of Southern Boulevard) just a couple blocks to the west, Georgia Avenue offers an edgier shopping environment in warehouses, lofts, and auction houses. Most notably, Kofski's Estate Sale Facility (5501 Georgia Ave.) has been handling some of the most important estate sales in the area since 1939 and has a nearly continuous collection of inventory available to purchase.

NORTHWOOD VILLAGE
northwoodvillage.com

This small charming district offers an eclectic mix of galleries, furniture, antiques, and accessories shops. On the second Sunday of each month, guided tours and special activities are part of the Northwood Art Walk.

SOUTH FLORIDA FAIRGROUNDS
wpbaf.com

The West Palm Beach Antiques Festival is held on the first weekend of every month and is one of the largest, regularly scheduled antiques shows in the south. The February extravaganza features 1,000 vendors.

Spas in Palm Beach & Vicinity

 If you are not already staying at one of the famous luxury resort hotels in Palm Beach with an in-house spa, it is possible (and highly recommended) to enjoy the services as a day visitor to any one of the numerous local spas. For a complete list of spa and wellness venues throughout the region, go to thepalmbeaches.com/spas-wellness. Here is a short list of the area's best-known spas:

THE SPA AT THE BREAKERS
One S. County Rd., Palm Beach, FL 33480; (561) 655-6611, thebreakers.com

After an $8 million renovation, the Spa at the Breakers is considered to be world class. The calming design incorporates the calming virtues of the seaside location and Italian-influenced architecture into a relaxed, modern space. Extensive indoor/outdoor amenities and services include hair and nail services,

3 dedicated lounges, and a private, coed courtyard. The spa offers specialty Tammy Fender, OSEA, and ERBE treatments, and customized massages.

EAU PALM BEACH RESORT & SPA
100 S. Ocean Blvd., Manalapan, FL 33462; (561) 533-6000; eaupalmbeach.com

With a 42,000-square-foot indoor/outdoor spa wonderland, Eau Spa features 19 treatment rooms with customized scents, music, and lighting; Self-Centered Garden complete with dipping pools, hanging chairs, cabanas, and massage bench; private Garden Villas with outdoor showers, bathtubs, and lounging area; Scrub & Polish Bars; bath lounges; saunas; steam rooms; fitness center; oversized Jacuzzis; and much more.

The Self-Centered Garden at Eau Palm Beach Resort & Spa. Photo courtesy of Eau Palm Beach Resort & Spa

KEY TO LIFE MED SPA
270 S. County Rd., Palm Beach, FL 33480; (561) 655-1000; keytolifemedspa.com

Located on Palm Beach Island, the Key to Life Med Spa is a premier upscale medical spa offering a complete medical, cosmetic, and spa experience, providing a combination of antiaging medicine, laser treatments, nutrition, and relaxation.

ANUSHKA SPA, SALON & COSMEDICAL CENTRE
701 S. Rosemary Ave. (CityPlace), West Palm Beach, FL 33401; (561) 820-0500; anushkaspa.com

This highly acclaimed "med spa" features 12,000 square feet of space, with a hair salon, spa sanctuary, cellulite clinic, cosmedical center, and bridal beauty loft.

KAFFEE'S GARDEN SPA
4100 S. Dixie Hwy., West Palm Beach, FL 33405; (561) 833-4483; kaffeesgardenspa.com

A nice, low-key alternative to the larger exclusive spas, the highly acclaimed Kaffee's Garden Spa offers a charming environment with extensive services, including dry salt therapy, hair care, facials, massages, body waxing, and more.

Guanabanas offers a tropical dining experience.

CHAPTER 7

EAT, DRINK & BE MERRY

As one of the oldest resorts in the United States, the Palm Beach area has had a long tradition in hospitality and the culinary arts. In addition to the exclusive and fine dining establishments on Palm Beach Island, the city of West Palm Beach has a vibrant, creative restaurant scene gaining regional and national attention.

Of course, the opinions about restaurants are generally subjective, and it would be possible to write a book just about restaurants in the Palm Beaches. Therefore, the directory below is only a short list of proven restaurants on Palm Beach Island and the immediate vicinity with a few regional standouts included as well. The list is by no means comprehensive and is meant to be a basic guide for visitors. Restaurants that are waterfront or offer a water view have been marked with an asterisk (*).

Fine Dining on Palm Beach Island

Cocktail attire or Palm Beach Chic would be appropriate for these restaurants.

CAFÉ L'EUROPE

331 S. County Rd., Palm Beach, FL 33480; (561) 655-4020; cafeleurope.com

Iconic Palm Beach fine-dining establishment with a vibrant atmosphere and live piano music. Great for celebrity watching. Dinner only.

BISTRO CHEZ JEAN-PIERRE

132 N. County Rd., Palm Beach, FL 33480; (561) 833-1171; chezjean-pierre.com

Consistently one of the most highly rated fine-dining restaurants in Palm Beach County. Dinner only.

RENATO'S

87 Via Mizner, Palm Beach, FL 33480; (561) 655-9752; renatospalmbeach.com

With its enchanting location in Via Mizner off Worth Avenue, this is one of the most romantic, fine-dining restaurants in Palm Beach with nice outdoor dining. Italian cuisine. Lunch and dinner served. Palm Beach Casual for lunch, otherwise cocktail attire.

CAFÉ BOULUD

The Brazilian Court, 301 Australian Ave., Palm Beach, FL 33480; (561) 655-6060; cafeboulud.com/palmbeach

Famous chef Daniel Boulud has created this highly rated fine-dining French restaurant, which also features charming outdoor dining in a courtyard. Breakfast, lunch, and dinner. Palm Beach Casual for lunch, otherwise cocktail attire in the evening.

SANT AMBROEUS

340 Royal Poinciana Way (Royal Poinciana Plaza), Palm Beach, FL 33480; (561) 285-7990; santambroeus.com

A chic, very trendy Italian restaurant offering breakfast, lunch, and dinner as well as a vibrant bar with a popular cocktail hour. You can dine in the formal dining room or at the casual high and low tables facing the bar. Takeout counter also available with gourmet items and gift baskets. Palm Beach Casual in the bar.

Other Upscale Restaurants & Grills on the Island

Palm Beach Chic or Palm Beach Casual would be appropriate for any of these restaurants.

PALM BEACH GRILL
340 Royal Poinciana Way, Palm Beach, FL 33480; (561) 835-1077; palmbeachgrill.com

A mainstay in Palm Beach and nearly impossible to get a reservation (taken maximum 30 days in advance), but you can often get a seat at the bar. Excellent grill, dinner only.

BUCCAN
350 S. County Rd., Palm Beach, FL 33480; (561) 833-3450; buccanpalmbeach.com

Trendy, upscale Palm Beach eclectic eatery popular with the younger jet set. Chef Clay Conley's innovative menu offers a wonderful selection of smaller dishes as well. The main dining room serves dinner only, but the Sandwich Shop offers lunch featuring counter-service pressed and cold artisan sandwiches, fresh salads, sides, and sweets. All breads are made in-house.

IMOTO AT BUCCAN
350 S. County Rd., Palm Beach, FL 33401; (561) 833-5522; imotopalmbeach.com

Located immediately adjacent to Buccan, Chef Clay Conley has created a popular Asian-themed restaurant offering menu items influenced by Japanese and other Asian flavors.

TA-BOO
221 Worth Ave., Palm Beach, FL 33480; (561) 835-3500; taboorestaurant.com

Legendary Palm Beach "classic" for over 75 years serving "new American" cuisine on Worth Avenue. The place to see and be seen for lunch, with a popular bar that makes it a well-known watering hole. Lunch and dinner.

BICE
313 Worth Ave., Palm Beach, FL 33480; (561) 835-1600; bice-palmbeach.com

Another Palm Beach stalwart serving fine Italian cuisine on Worth Avenue and featuring nice al fresco dining for lunch and dinner.

BRICKTOP'S
375 S. County Rd., Palm Beach, FL 33480; (561) 855-2030; bricktops.com/palm-beach

One of Palm Beach's newest grill restaurants with consistently high ratings. Lunch and dinner with outdoor dining available.

CHEZ L' EPICIER
288 S. County Rd., Palm Beach, FL 33480; (561) 508-7030; chezlepicier.com

Set in a French Country décor offering an inventive, diverse menu with something for everyone. The signature (complimentary) appetizer macarons are a special added touch and the popular, very moderately priced Thursday night mussel special includes endless servings of Prince Edward Island mussels and french fries. The Palm Beach Chamber of Commerce awarded this restaurant "best new business" in 2017.

COSTA PALM BEACH
150 Worth Ave., # 234, Palm Beach, FL 33480; (561) 429-8456

Located within the elegant Esplanade on Worth Avenue offering Mediterranean dishes with a focus on the classics with a modern twist. The clam bake special for parties of four on Tuesdays is a great deal (it also includes lobster, mussels, and Alaskan king crab). Complimentary dinner valet.

HMF
The Breakers Palm Beach, 1 S. County Rd., Palm Beach, FL 33480; (561) 290-0104; thebreakers.com

HMF is an abbreviation for Henry Morrison Flagler, the founder of the Breakers. The restaurant was completely revamped by celebrated hospitality designer Adam D. Tihany. Great for people watching in the opulent setting of the Breakers, serving classic cocktails and a creative menu of small plates that are high-end takes on American fare, sushi, Italian favorites, and global street food. Don't forget to get your parking ticket validated! Dinner only.

FLAGLER STEAKHOUSE
2 S. County Rd., Palm Beach, FL 33480; (855) 435-2053; thebreakers.com

A Breakers satellite steakhouse overlooking the 18th hole, with the West Palm Beach skyline in the distance, has a clubby atmosphere. Pricey but large portions are great for sharing. Lunch and dinner (well known for great lunch deals).

MEAT MARKET
191 Bradley Place, Palm Beach, FL 33480; (561) 354-9800; meatmarket.net

Featuring a contemporary ambience, this is a very popular and rather expensive beef lover's paradise with top-quality steaks and creative steak butters and sauces. Busy bar scene out front. Dinner only.

TREVINI RISTORANTE

290 Sunset Ave., Palm Beach, FL 33480; (561) 833-3883; treviniristorante.com

A charming Italian restaurant with a contemporary feel inside and romantic dining outside around a fountain in the brick courtyard. Excellent food and wine list. Lunch and dinner.

ECHO PALM BEACH

230 Sunrise Ave., Palm Beach, FL 33480; (855) 435-0061; echopalmbeach.com

Featuring a lively bar with "pan-Asian" cuisine, including very good sushi. Popular with the trendy set. Dinner only.

PB CATCH

251 Sunrise Ave., Palm Beach, FL 33480; (561) 655-5558; pbcatch.com

High-quality seafood served in a contemporary nautical-themed setting. Famous for the oysters. Dinner only.

*CHARLEY'S CRAB

456 S. Ocean Blvd., Palm Beach, FL 33480; (561) 659-1500

Well-established upscale (without being pretentious) seafood restaurant with an ocean view. Serving lunch and dinner, with a popular brunch on Sundays.

*THE SEAFOOD BAR

The Breakers Palm Beach, 1 S. County Rd., Palm Beach, FL 33480; (561) 290-0104; thebreakers.com

Located at The Breakers and open for lunch and dinner, this popular oceanfront restaurant and raw bar features fresh fish, clams, oysters, lobster, shrimp, and chowders.

Casual Restaurants on the Island

Palm Beach Casual or even Casual would be appropriate for these restaurants.

LA CUCINA (FORMERLY CUCINA DELL' ARTE)

257 Royal Poinciana Way, Palm Beach, FL 33480; (561) 655-0770;
cucinadellarte.com

The restaurant is due to reopen with a refreshed design and concept. Serving breakfast, lunch, and dinner, this casual trendy Italian restaurant is particularly popular with younger Palm Beachers later in the evening, when it turns into a lounge for mingling and dancing.

PIZZA AL FRESCO

14 Via Mizner (off Worth Ave.), Palm Beach, FL 33480; (561) 832-0032;
pizzaalfresco.com

One of the inside tips for an affordable, romantic lunch or dinner in Palm Beach. Casual, outdoor dining in a secluded courtyard serving the best pizza in Palm Beach County (thin Italian-style crusts).

CAFÉ FLORA

240 Worth Ave., Palm Beach, FL 33480; (561) 514-4959; cafeviaflora.com

Another inside tip for casual, outdoor, affordable dining for lunch or dinner in another charming Worth Avenue courtyard.

SURFSIDE DINER

314 S. County Rd., Palm Beach, FL 33480; (561) 659-7495

Palm Beach's popular diner serving quality breakfast and lunch.

GREEN'S LUNCHEONETTE AT GREEN'S PHARMACY

151 N. County Rd., Palm Beach, FL 33480; (561) 832-4443

A legendary mainstay in Palm Beach, visitors step back into time at this authentic pharmacy luncheonette, serving breakfast and lunch.

*AL FRESCO AT THE PALM BEACH PAR 3 GOLF COURSE

2345 S. Ocean Blvd., Palm Beach, FL 33480; (561) 547-0598; alfrescopb.com

The sister restaurant of Pizza al Fresco on Worth Avenue, Al Fresco Ristorante/ Bar is located at the Par 3 Golf Course clubhouse and features spectacular ocean views and the surrounding golf course. Breakfast, lunch, and dinner.

Dinner & Dancing on the Island

Palm Beach Chic or Palm Beach Casual would be appropriate for these venues, depending on the time of the year.

POLO STEAKHOUSE RESTAURANT

The Colony Palm Beach, 155 Hammon Ave., Palm Beach, FL 33480; (561) 655-5430; thecolonypalmbeach.com

Upscale hotel steakhouse offering a surf 'n' turf menu and tableside cooking, plus poolside seating. Regularly featuring live music, including the always popular "Motown Friday Nights" with lots of dancing.

LEOPARD LOUNGE & RESTAURANT

The Chesterfield Palm Beach, 363 Cocoanut Row, Palm Beach, FL 33480; (561) 659-5800; chesterfieldpb.com

Wonderful old-school food and service, popular with locals and hotel guests alike for dancing to live music until the wee hours of the night. This is where the ladies and gentlemen go to meet. Breakfast, lunch, and dinner.

Dinner Cabaret

THE ROYAL ROOM

The Colony Palm Beach, 155 Hammon Ave., Palm Beach, FL 33480; (561) 655-5430; theroyalroom.com

One of the most elegant, sophisticated, and intimate dinner cabarets in the United States, the Royal Room is very special to Palm Beach. Dinner only on show nights. Subject to availability, it is also possible to attend a show without dinner.

Markets with Prepared Food & Takeout Options on the Island

C'EST SI BON GOURMET SHOP
280 Sunset Ave., Palm Beach, FL 33480; (561) 659-6503; csbgourmet.com

Gourmet to go, grocery, gift baskets, and catering.

AMICI MARKET
155 N. County Rd., Palm Beach, FL 33480; (561) 832-0201

Gourmet to go (also ideal for a dinner party) and groceries.

PUBLIX SUPER MARKET ON PALM BEACH
135 Bradley Place, Palm Beach, FL 33480; (561) 655-4120

The only supermarket on the island, this is considered to be the nicest Publix in the entire company, complete with a deli, meat and seafood counters, prepared meals, an extensive selection of wines, and, of course, valet parking!

THE SANDWICH SHOP
350 S. County Rd., Palm Beach, FL 33480; (561) 833-6295

Operated by restaurant Buccan (located on the side of the restaurant).

BLUE PROVENCE
300 S. County Road, Palm Beach, FL 33480; (561) 249-0522;blueprovence.com

French gourmet, Balik salmon, cavier, tablewares, and delicious sandwiches.

PATRICK LEZE
229 Sunrise Ave., Palm Beach, FL 33480; (561) 366-1313; patrickleze.com

This authentic French bakery offers breakfast, lunch, and fresh-from-the-oven delights, such as croissants, macarons, cream puffs, and tortes. Sandwiches and salads are also delicious.

SPRINKLES ICE CREAM & SANDWICH SHOP
279 Royal Poinciana Way, Palm Beach, FL 33480; (561) 659-1140

The best ice cream on the island! Also offers light fare and burgers.

Off the Island: West Palm Beach

UPSCALE RESTAURANTS

Palm Beach Casual would be appropriate for these restaurants (although jackets are less common in the summer).

TABLE 26

1700 S. Dixie Hwy., West Palm Beach, FL 33401; (561) 835-2660; table26palmbeach.com

A highly rated restaurant serving globally influenced American cuisine. Popular with the Palm Beach crowd as well, so be sure to make a reservation. The outside terrace is very pleasant during the cooler months. Dinner and lunch served Monday through Saturday, and on Sundays they serve an outstanding brunch. Try the delicious Table 26 Signature Martini!

*PISTACHE

101 N. Clematis St., West Palm Beach, FL 33401; (561) 833-5090; pistachewpb.com

The most popular French brasserie restaurant in the area. Al fresco dining with partial views to the Lake Worth Lagoon.

KITCHEN

319 Belvedere Rd., West Palm Beach, FL 33405; (561) 249-2281; kitchenpb.com

Highly rated "new American brasserie" for foodies seeking seasonal creations. Very small intimate dining with just two seatings in the evening, so make reservations.

LA SIRENA

6316 S. Dixie Hwy., West Palm Beach, FL 33405; (561) 585-3128; lasirenaonline.com

A West Palm Beach venerable restaurant serving fine Italian cuisine on white tablecloths and featuring an extensive wine cellar. Dinner only.

THE REGIONAL KITCHEN & PUBLIC HOUSE

651 Okeechobee Blvd., West Palm Beach, FL 33401; (561) 557-6460; eatregional.com

Hailed as one of the best new restaurants in 2016, this restaurant boasts one of the area's first farm-to-table concepts. Outdoor dining available.

OKEECHOBEE STEAKHOUSE

2854 Okeechobee Blvd., West Palm Beach, FL 33409; (561) 683-5151; okeechobeesteakhouse.com

The granddaddy of local steakhouses (nearly 70 years in business) offering superb steaks and great cocktails (with separate lounge) in a dimly lit atmosphere (popular with locals). Lunch and dinner.

POPULAR, TRENDY & MODERATELY PRICED

LYNORA'S
207 Clematis St., West Palm Beach, FL 33401; (561) 899-3117; lynoras.com

Popular casual Italian restaurant. Lunch and dinner.

AVOCADO GRILL
125 Datura St., West Palm Beach, FL 33401; (561) 623-0822; avocadogrillwpb.com

New American bistro with a whole section on the menu devoted to the restaurant's namesake fruit (guac, yes, but also grilled avocado wedges, and so on), in addition to veggies, sushi, seafood, and land-based protein. Rustic, charming, urban atmosphere. Lunch and dinner.

HULLABALOO
517 Clematis St., West Palm Beach, FL 33401; (561) 833-1033; sub-culture.org/hullabaloo

Popular Italian gastropub on Clematis Street with a retro look. A charming urban feel with outdoor dining and a restored Airstream camper great for groups in the back patio. Lunch and dinner (turning into more of a bar late at night).

ROCCO'S TACOS & TEQUILA BAR
224 Clematis St., West Palm Beach, FL 33401; (561) 650-1001; roccostacos.com

Very popular Mexican restaurant with great margaritas and guacamole made tableside. Lunch and dinner.

IL BELLAGIO
600 S. Rosemary Ave. (CityPlace), West Palm Beach, FL 33401; (561) 659-6160; ilbellagiocityplace.com

Highly rated Italian cuisine that is moderately priced. Featuring an expansive terrace overlooking the main plaza water fountains, this is a consistently good choice while visiting CityPlace. Lunch and dinner.

CITY CELLAR WINE BAR & GRILL
700 S. Rosemary Ave., West Palm Beach, FL 33401; (561) 366-0071; citycellarwpb.com

Consistent, popular, moderately priced grill restaurant at West Palm's CityPlace that has "something for everyone." Expansive terrace for sitting outside. Lunch and dinner.

GRATO

1901 S. Dixie Hwy., West Palm Beach, FL 33401; (561) 404-1334; gratowpb.com

A trendy, vibrant Italian pizzeria serving lunch and dinner, with an excellent brunch on Sundays.

RHYTHM CAFÉ

3800A S. Dixie Hwy., West Palm Beach, FL 33405; (561) 833-3406; rhythmcafe.com

Very popular funky and eclectic American bistro. Diverse menu, fish offerings excellent. Dinner only.

DARBSTER

8020 S. Dixie Hwy., West Palm Beach, FL 33405; (561) 586-2622; darbster.com

Outstanding vegan menu featuring some raw dishes and gluten-free items in a casual atmosphere. Dinner only except Sunday when they serve brunch.

HAVANA

6801 S. Dixie Hwy., West Palm Beach, FL 33405; (561) 547-9799; havanacubanfood.com

A popular family-friendly cantina serving Cuban fare. There is also a very popular 24/7 to-go window. Lunch and dinner only.

CAFÉ CENTRO

2409 N. Dixie Hwy., West Palm Beach, FL 33407; (561) 514-4070; cafecentrowpb.com

Northwood Road. Lunch and dinner.

SUNSET BAR & GRILL

2500 Broadway, West Palm Beach, FL 33407; (561) 832-2722; eatatsunset.com

Charming, casual American fare served in an eclectic, art-filled space with a patio. Popular with locals; serves dinner only with a nice cocktail bar.

CASUAL & SPECIALTY RESTAURANTS & PUBS IN WEST PALM BEACH

*E.R. BRADLEY'S

104 N. Clematis St., West Palm Beach, FL 33401 (enter restaurant on Datura); (561) 833-3520; erbradleys.com

A landmark bar and restaurant on the West Palm Beach waterfront, this casual sports bar/restaurant is known for its outside dining with views across the Intracoastal Waterway. Breakfast, lunch, and dinner.

JOY NOODLES & RICE

2200 S. Dixie Hwy., West Palm Beach, FL 33401; (561) 655-5212; joynoodles.net

A casual locals' hangout offering some of the best Thai/Pan-Asian fare in the area at very reasonable prices. Lunch and dinner.

KABUKI SUSHI THAI TAPAS

308 N. Clematis St., West Palm Beach, FL 33401; (561) 833-6349; kabukiwpb.com

Great sushi with inventive combos and tasty Thai dishes. Lunch and dinner.

BELLE & MAXWELL'S

3700 S. Dixie Hwy., West Palm Beach, FL 33405; (561) 832-4449; belleandmaxwells.com

Homey teahouse/café with a garden patio offering a casual Mediterranean-inspired menu. Lunch and dinner.

SERENITY TEA GARDEN & RESTAURANT

316 Vallette Way, West Palm Beach, FL 33401; (561) 655-3911; serenitygardentea.com

Traditional afternoon tea, plus sandwiches and light fare, served in nostalgic, charming antique-filled rooms. Lunch and afternoon tea.

QUEEN OF SHEEBA

716 N. Sapodilla Ave., West Palm Beach, FL 33401; (561) 514-0615; queenofsheebawpb.com

Located in the Northwest Historic District and offering contemporary dishes featuring authentic Ethiopian flavors with local and imported ingredients. Lunch and dinner.

INDUS

1649 Forum Place, Ste 6-7, West Palm Beach, FL 33401; (561) 249-0123; indusdine.com

Located in an ugly strip mall hidden behind office towers, this restaurant prepares the best Indian food in the area. Lunch and dinner.

COFFEE SHOPS, BAKERIES & DINERS

SUBCULTURE COFFEE
509 Clematis St., West Palm Beach, FL 33401; (561) 318-5142; subculturecoffee.com

A trendy coffee shop open until late (2 a.m. on the weekends, otherwise midnight). Excellent coffee and very nice bakery goods as well. Outdoor seating available.

JOHAN'S JOE
401 S. Dixie Hwy. #3, West Palm Beach, FL 33401; (561) 808-5090; johansjoe.com

A very popular addition to downtown West Palm Beach's coffee culture also offering breakfast and lunch (closes early evening). Swedish themed. Try the pancakes!

PANETERIE
205 Clematis St., West Palm Beach, FL 33401; (561) 233-2992; paneterie.com

Offering some of the best French pastries around as well as breakfast and lunch. The macaroons are incredible and there is a nice selection of high-quality coffee and tea. Outdoor seating available.

PARIS BAKERY & CAFÉ
212 S. Olive Ave., West Palm Beach, FL 33401; (561) 820-9281; parisbakerycafe.com

Small café serving sweet and savory crêpes, sandwiches, salads, and soups, also with outdoor seating. Try the delicious almond or chocolate croissants.

HOWLEY'S
4700 S. Dixie Hwy., West Palm Beach, FL 33405; (561) 833-5691; sub-culture.org/howleys

Since 1950, the motto of this legendary, midcentury diner has been "Cooked in sight, must be right." Comfort chow amid 1950s decor with a pressed-tin ceiling, full bar, and jukebox. Open until 2 a.m. during the week and 5 a.m. on the weekends.

TULIPAN BAKERY
740 Belvedere Rd., West Palm Beach, FL 33405; (561) 832-6107; tulipanbakery.com

Local legendary Cuban coffee shop also offering baked sweets and sandwiches.

Other Noteworthy Regional Restaurants

*SAILFISH MARINA RESTAURANT
Sailfish Marina Resort, 98 Lake Dr., Palm Beach Shores, FL 33404; (561) 842-8449; sailfishmarina.com/restaurant

One of the most charming waterfront restaurants in the area with lovely sunsets, specializing in Florida seafood. Take a walk along the docks while waiting for your table and see all the fish in the crystal-clear water. Breakfast, lunch, and dinner. Outdoor seating available.

*U TIKI BEACH
1095 N. H A1A, Jupiter, FL 33477; (561) 406-2210; utikibeach.com

Caribbean food and drinks in a casual island setting with deck and beach seating and spectacular water views toward the Jupiter Lighthouse. Try to get here about 1 hour before sunset. Dinner only on weekdays with lunch served also on weekends. Indoor and outdoor seating.

*JETTY'S WATERFRONT RESTAURANT
1075 N. H A1A, Jupiter, FL 33477; (561) 743-8166; jettysjupiter.com

Very popular, upscale family-friendly restaurant with views of the Jupiter Lighthouse and a menu of just-caught seafood. Try to get here at least 1 hour before sunset. Dinner only. Indoor/outdoor seating.

*GUANABANAS RESTAURANT
960 N. H A1A, Jupiter, FL 33477; (561) 747-8878; guanabanas.com

Diners can enjoy live music and exclusively local seafood in a romantic, open-air setting directly on the water. The wait for a table can be enjoyed by sipping on a cocktail down by the water in one of the many lounge chairs. Get here an hour before sunset. Lunch and dinner during the week and also serving breakfast on the weekends.

*CAFFE LUNA ROSA
34 S. Ocean Blvd., Delray Beach, FL 33483; (561) 274-9404; caffelunarosa.com

There are many good restaurants in Delray Beach along Atlantic Avenue, but this popular Italian bistro boasts views toward the ocean and has won many accolades for its food. Serves breakfast, lunch, and dinner.

SUNDY HOUSE
106 Swinton Ave., Delray Beach, FL 33444; (561) 272-5678; sundyhouse.com

Eclectic dining pavilions set within a lush botanical garden of tropical plants. Dinner plus brunch on Saturday and Sunday.

Cocktail Hour & Nightlife

Following a tradition that started during the Gilded Age on the veranda of the old Royal Poinciana Hotel overlooking the Lake Worth Lagoon, Palm Beach has always been famous for cocktail hour leading up to sunset. During the Season, whether private, public, or for charity, there are cocktail parties and similar gatherings going on all over town every night.

The tradition has spilled over to the entire region. Cocktail hour is typically finished by 8:30 p.m.—and when most towns in the area are relatively quiet, the city of West Palm Beach becomes the main destination for partiers. Here is a short list of great places to enjoy drinks during cocktail hour and a few suggestions for late-night reveling.

COCKTAIL BARS, WINE BARS & MICRO BREWERIES ON THE ISLAND

HMF

The Breakers Palm Beach, 1 S. County Rd., Palm Beach, FL 33480; (561) 290-0104; thebreakers.com

HMF is an abbreviation for Henry Morrison Flagler, the founder of the Breakers. The restaurant was completely revamped by celebrated hospitality designer Adam D. Tihany. Great for people watching in the opulent setting of the Breakers, serving classic cocktails and a creative menu of small plates that are high-end takes on American fare, sushi, Italian favorites, and global street food. Don't forget to get your parking ticket validated! Dinner only.

LEOPARD LOUNGE

The Chesterfield Palm Beach, 363 Cocoanut Row, Palm Beach, FL 33480; (561) 659-5800; chesterfieldpb.com

Popular with locals and hotel guests alike for both cocktail hour and dancing to live music until the wee hours of the morning, the Leopard Bar is where the ladies and gentlemen go to meet. Happy Hour Sunday through Thursday between 4:30 and 6:30 p.m. Jackets recommended.

LA CUCINA (FORMERLY CUCINA DELL' ARTE)

257 Royal Poinciana Way, Palm Beach, FL 33480; (561) 655-0770; cucinadellarte.com

The restaurant is due to reopen with a refreshed design and concept. Serving breakfast, lunch, and dinner, this casual, trendy Italian restaurant is particularly popular with younger Palm Beachers later in the evening, when it turns into a lounge for mingling and dancing.

MEAT MARKET

191 Bradley Place, Palm Beach, FL 33480; (561) 354-9800

Relaxed, yet vibrant bar where friends meet. Can be quite crowded on weekends.

SANT AMBROEUS

340 Royal Poinciana Way (Royal Poinciana Plaza), Palm Beach, FL 33401; (561) 285-7990; santambroeus.com

A chic bar with wonderful cocktails. Very trendy.

THE POLO LOUNGE

The Colony Palm Beach, 155 Hammon Ave., Palm Beach, FL 33480; (561) 655-5430

A lovely gathering point for cocktails for all before heading out to dinner, the Polo Lounge is particularly popular with Palm Beach's gay gentlemen's scene on Thursday nights. Jackets are recommended.

COCKTAIL BARS, WINE BARS & MICROBREWERIES OFF THE ISLAND

THE BLUE MARTINI

550 S Rosemary Ave. (CityPlace), West Palm Beach, FL 33401; (561) 835-8601

This CityPlace hotspot is always bustling, attracting a steady crowd of upscale professionals and tourists. Behind the bar, musicians perform on an elevated stage against a grid of blue-lit cubbyholes playing Top 40 tunes, Latin music, '70s disco, and more with a small dance floor adjacent. An outdoor bar serves those who want to watch foot-traffic. Appetizers and desserts are available to supplement the booze, and fashionable attire is expected (but no jackets).

COPPER BLUES ROCK PUB & KITCHEN

550 S. Rosemary Ave. (CityPlace), West Palm Beach, FL 33401; (561) 404-4101

Copper Blues is a brewpub located on the second floor of CityPlace (next to Improv). The more than 60 beers on tap (mix of local crafts, microbrews, IPAs, and more) complement the scrumptious bar bites, burgers, etc. They have a stage in the center of the place that draws some of the hottest local rock and blues acts. Acts are typically booked for Wednesday through Saturday and posted on the website. Casual.

THE BLIND MONK

410 Evernia St. #107, West Palm Beach, FL 33401; (561) 833-3605

Chic, dimly lit tapas bar specializing in a large selection of affordable wines and small bites. Outdoor seating available. Casual.

IMPROV COMEDY CLUB

550 S. Rosemary Ave., #250, West Palm Beach, FL 33401; (561) 833-1812; palmbeach.improv.com

The Improv Comedy Club is a nationwide chain that has a spectacular, expansive location in West Palm Beach's CityPlace. The venue brings in top-name acts, including the likes of Sinbad, Tracy Morgan, and Bob Saget. Delicious cocktails are available as well as simple dinner food. If you like to laugh, go here! Casual.

THE ALCHEMIST GASTROPUB & BAR

223 Clematis St., West Palm Beach, FL 33401; (561) 355-0691; thealchemistgastropub.com

A cozy, urban pub atmosphere with a popular happy hour from 4 to 7 p.m. offering craft cocktails and above average pub food (including outstanding steaks!). Casual.

ROXY'S PUB

309 N. Clematis St., West Palm Beach, FL 33401; (561) 296-7699

Roxy's is a multistoried, multifaceted Irish pub and nightclub located right in the center of West Palm Beach's popular Clematis Street. On the bottom floor, sports and drinking fans gather to watch Florida sports teams take on the opposition. Up on the roof deck, you can look out over the city after grabbing a drink at one of the two bar stations. Later in the evening, house music blasts and music videos play on the projection screen. A pretty wild dance party usually ensues. Very casual.

O'SHEA'S IRISH PUB

531 Clematis St., West Palm Beach, FL 33401; (561) 833-3865; osheaspub.com

A perennial favorite for locals in the most charming section of Clematis Street. Live music, pool tables, great happy hours, and pub food.

H.G. ROOSTERS

823 Belvedere Rd., West Palm Beach, FL 33405; (561) 832-9119; roosterswpb.com

The oldest and most established gay bar in Palm Beach County (also the oldest in Florida!) with a friendly atmosphere, pool table, outdoor patio, and drag shows on the weekend. This bar is Cheers for the LGBTQ community—"where everybody knows your name."

NIGHTCLUBS

Although the Palm Beach area is not known for large-scale, mega-nightclubs as in Miami or Fort Lauderdale, there is plenty to do in downtown West Palm Beach, mainly on or around Clematis Street. The "in" club changes every season, but below is a short list of well-established clubs.

PAWN SHOP LOUNGE

219 Clematis St., West Palm Beach, FL 33401; (561) 833-6500; pawnshopwpb.com

Large scale, multifaceted 9,000-square-foot dance club attracting all age groups, located in the busiest section of Clematis Street in downtown West Palm Beach.

RESPECTABLE STREET

518 Clematis St., West Palm Beach, FL 33401; (561) 832-9999; sub-culture.org/respectable-street

The perennial favorite dance club for the younger set since 1987. This club was part of the initial revival of Clematis Street.

CAMELOT

114 S. Narcissus Ave., West Palm Beach, FL 33401; (561) 318-7675; sub-culture.org/camelot

This dance club is a homage to the Kennedys' love of the ocean, sailing, and Palm Beach.

CHAPTER 8

MAJOR ANNUAL EVENTS

Due to the increased number of residents during the season and the pleasant weather during fall, winter, and spring, most major events in the Palm Beach area occur from November 1 to May 1. There are many reoccurring smaller events taking place on a weekly basis, such as local farmers' markets, antiques markets, and historic home and garden tours. The overview compiled here includes only the largest annual events. Ask your hotel concierge for more suggestions or go to thepalmbeaches.com. There is likely to be something to satisfy every interest.

Consult websites for current dates, times, and other pertinent information.

RICK'S TIPS As a major supplier of fruit and vegetables during the fall, winter, and spring months, Palm Beach County is one of the most important agricultural counties in the United States. As a result, one of the most enjoyable activities in the area during those months is a visit to one of the many local farmers' markets. Most notably, the West Palm Beach GreenMarket is the area's first and premier green market located on the scenic downtown West Palm Beach Waterfront. Taking place every Saturday from 9 a.m. to 1 p.m. from October through April, the market showcases more than 80 vendors featuring the freshest and most unique offerings including local produce, plants, exotic flowers, herbs, baked goods, gourmet foods, teas, coffee, and more. The atmosphere is vibrant with live music, unlimited mimosas for $10, free activities for kids, plus lots of green space and seating for a morning of fun and relaxation.

JANUARY

Winter Equestrian Festival
Palm Beach International Equestrian Center, Wellington

The largest equestrian event in the United States (see page 99). January–April (561) 793-5867, pbiec.coth.com

Global Dressage Festival
Palm Beach International Equestrian Center, Wellington

The largest dressage circuit in the world (see page 99). January–April. (561) 793-5867, gdf.coth.com

Polo Tournaments
International Polo Club Palm Beach, Wellington

(see page 101). January (first Sunday)–April (fourth Sunday). (561) 282-5334, internationalpoloclub.com

Palm Beach Modern & Contemporary
West Palm Beach

Organized by the well-established Art Miami, this show has quickly become an important date on the calendar of art enthusiasts. First half of January every year. Artpbfair.com

ArtPalmBeach
Palm Beach County Convention Center, West Palm Beach

A major art show focusing on contemporary art. Held for 4-5 days in mid-late January. artpalmbeach.com

South Florida Fair
South Florida Fairgrounds, West Palm Beach

One of the oldest, largest, and top-rated fairs in Florida. Runs 17 days every January. (561) 793-0333, southfloridafair.com

FOTOfusion
Palm Beach Photographic Centre, West Palm Beach

International festival of photography and digital imaging. Held in late January each year. (561) 253-2600, fotofusion.org

FEBRUARY

West Palm Beach Antiques Festival Extravaganza
South Florida Fairgrounds, West Palm Beach

1,000 vendors. First weekend of February. (941) 697-7475; wpbaf.com

Delray Beach Open
Delray Beach

Major ATP Champions Tour Event and ATP World Tour Event. Mid-February. yellowtennisball.com

Palm Beach Jewelry
Art & Antique Fair, Palm Beach County Convention Center, West Palm Beach

One of the largest jewelry, art, and antique fairs in the country. palmbeachshow.com

ArtiGras Fine Arts Festival
Jupiter

Popular 3-day, family-friendly event celebrating art in all media types, as well as live music and food. Presidents Day weekend. (561) 746-7111, artigras.org

Street Painting Festival
Lake Worth

Very popular 2-day event, with many works completed by the second day. Visiting in the morning lets you avoid walking on the pavement beneath the hot sun. streetpaintingfestivalinc.org

The Honda Classic
PGA National Resort & Spa, Palm Beach Gardens

The region's most significant annual golf tournament. thehondaclassic.com

Winter Equestrian Festival
Palm Beach International Equestrian Center, Wellington

The largest equestrian event in the United States (see page 99). January–April. (561) 793-5867, pbiec.coth.com

Global Dressage Festival
Palm Beach International Equestrian Center, Wellington

The largest dressage circuit in the world (see page 99). January–April. (561) 793-5867, gdf.coth.com

Polo Tournaments
International Polo Club Palm Beach, Wellington (see page 101).

January (first Sunday)–April (fourth Sunday). (561) 282-5334, internationalpoloclub.com

MARCH

Evening on Antique Row
West Palm Beach

One of the major events of the Season, this is a vibrant street festival with entry to dozens of shops with entertainment and refreshments. (561) 832-4164, historicalsocietypbc.org

Palm Beach International Boat Show
West Palm Beach waterfront

One of the largest boat shows in the country. showmanagement.com

Pet Parade and Contest
Palm Beach

The Island's finest four-footed friends and their owners dress up. (561) 659-6909, worth-avenue.com

PrideFest of the Palm Beaches
Bryant Park, Lake Worth

Largest LGBTQ event in the region—a 2-day event with a parade on Sunday morning. (561) 533-9699, compassglcc.com

St. Patrick's Day Parade & Festival
Delray Beach

The area's largest St. Patrick's Day celebration taking place on and around charming Atlantic Avenue. St. Patrick's Day weekend. stpatrickmarch.com

Boca Bacchanal

Boca Raton

A weekend of events with fabulous food and wonderful wine, paired and presented by celebrated chefs throughout Boca Raton. Usually end of March. bocabacchanal.com

Winter Equestrian Festival

Palm Beach International Equestrian Center, Wellington

The largest equestrian event in the United States (see page 99). January–April. (561) 793-5867, pbiec.coth.com

Global Dressage Festival

Palm Beach International Equestrian Center, Wellington

The largest dressage circuit in the world (see page 99). January–April. (561) 793-5867, gdf.coth.com

Polo Tournaments

International Polo Club Palm Beach, Wellington

(see page 101) January (first Sunday)– April (fourth Sunday). (561) 282-5334, internationalpoloclub.com

APRIL

Barrett-Jackson Auto Auction

South Florida Fairgrounds, West Palm Beach

Major collector car auction with events for car lovers. barrett-jackson.com

Gay Polo League Tournament

Wellington

A unique LGBTQ weekend of events starting with a kick-off party (Friday), Gay Polo Tournament on Saturday afternoon, followed by an after party (Saturday), and brunch at the International Polo Club (Sunday). (561) 753-3389, gaypolo.com

Winter Equestrian Festival

Palm Beach International Equestrian Center, Wellington

The largest equestrian event in the United States (see page 99). January–April. (561) 793-5867, pbiec.coth.com

Global Dressage Festival

Palm Beach International Equestrian Center, Wellington

The largest dressage circuit in the world (see page 99). January–April. (561) 793-5867, gdf.coth.com

Polo Tournaments

International Polo Club Palm Beach, Wellington

(see page 101). January (first Sunday)– April (fourth Sunday). (561) 282-5334, internationalpoloclub.com

MAY

SunFest

Downtown West Palm Beach

Florida's largest waterfront music and art festival, featuring major performing artists and attracting more than 275,000 visitors. First weekend May (sometimes beginning at the end of April). (800) 786-3378, sunfest.com

Mounts Botanical Garden Connoisseurs Garden Tour

West Palm Beach and countywide

A Mother's Day weekend tradition, this is arguably the nicest garden tour of the year. Mother's Day Weekend. (561) 822-1515, mounts.org

JUNE

Stonewall Ball Black and White Party
Harriet Himmel Theater, CityPlace,
West Palm Beach

The largest annual LGBTQ ball in the
Palm Beaches. Last Saturday in June.
(561) 533-9699, compassglcc.com

JULY

4th on Flagler
Downtown West Palm Beach
Waterfront

One of the largest July Fourth celebrations
in Florida, located directly on the waterfront. Food, music, fun, fireworks!
Fourth of July. (561) 822-1515, wpb.org

Shakespeare by the Sea
Carlin Park, Jupiter

Open-air production; bring own seating
or blanket and drinks and food, or
purchase them at event. (561) 762-8552,
pbshakespeare.org

Palm Beach Chamber Music Festival
West Palm Beach and countywide

Held on multiple dates. (561) 547-1070,
pbcmf.org

Palm Beach Summer Beer Fest
South Florida Fairgrounds,
West Palm Beach

palmbeachsummerbeerfest.com

SEPTEMBER

Flavor Palm Beach
Countywide

Palm Beach County's restaurant month;
participating restaurants present a selection of specially priced three-course meals
for lunch and dinner. The entire month of
September. flavorpb.com

OCTOBER

Oktoberfest
The American German Club of the
Palm Beaches, Lake Worth

One of the largest Oktoberfest celebrations in the country, taking place over
two weekends with authentic German
cuisine and music (from bands flown in
from Germany). (561) 967-6464,
americanger manclub.org

NOVEMBER

Canvas Outdoor Museum Show
Downtown West Palm Beach

Championing art in public places,
CANVAS transforms landscapes into an
interactive art experience and has become
one of the most important, unique art
events of the year in the Palm Beach area.
canvaswpb.org

Delray Beach Wine and Seafood Festival
Downtown Delray Beach

Two-day event on and around Atlantic
Avenue. (561) 279-0907,
dbwineandseafood.com

DECEMBER

West Palm Beach Arts Festival
West Palm Beach

Features local and out-of-town artists,
live music, demonstrations and activities
for all ages at the historically landmarked
Armory Art Center in West Palm Beach.
Meet the artists and browse through
their work including jewelry, ceramics,
sculpture, paintings, and drawings. First
weekend every December.(561) 832-1776,
westpalmbeachartsfestival.com

Christmas Tree Lighting
Worth Avenue. Palm Beach

Arrive early to get a good view; includes Santa, parade, some stores open, and the lighting of a Menorah. (561) 659-6909, worth-avenue.com

Christmas Tree Lighting
Waterfront Park, West Palm Beach

Sandi the Christmas Tree is sculpted from 600 tons of sand; smaller sand sculptures are on display around downtown. Map available. Month-long event. (561) 822-1515, wpb.org

Palm Beach Holiday Boat Parade
Intracoastal Waterway from North Palm Beach to Jupiter Inlet Lighthouse.

Holiday Boat Parades are a south Florida tradition and quite unique. (561) 863-0012, palmbeachboatparade.com

Palm Beach Food and Wine Festival
Various locations across Palm Beach Island and beyond

The area's most upscale food and wine festival. pbfoodwinefest.com

The Palm Beaches Marathon
West Palm Beach

The region's most significant marathon, includes the traditional half marathon and 5K races with water views. palmbeachesmarathon.com

Best Websites with Local Event Calendars:

The most important websites with calendar information about local cultural and social events are:

thepalmbeaches.com

thingstodo.palmbeachpost.com

palmbeachculture.com

palmbeachsports.com

palmbeachdailynews.com/society/social-calendar/

notables.palmbeachpost.com/calendar

LGBTQ Community: compassglcc.com

CHAPTER 9

LODGING

Hotels are clustered together into the following seven general areas: town of Palm Beach/Palm Beach Island, downtown West Palm Beach, Palm Beach International Airport and I-95 corridor, Jupiter, Palm Beach Gardens, Delray Beach, and Boca Raton. The most exclusive hotels are all located on Palm Beach Island, with the only exception being the beautiful Boca Raton Resort & Club. For a complete listing of all hotels in the region, go to thepalmbeaches.com/places-to-stay. Below is a short list of local lodging establishments.

Town of Palm Beach (Palm Beach Island)

THE BREAKERS PALM BEACH

1 S. County Rd., Palm Beach, FL 33480; (561) 655-6611; thebreakers.com

Featured extensively in this guide (see page 8), this is the most famous, historic, exclusive full-scale resort in Florida located directly on the ocean with a private beach.

THE COLONY PALM BEACH

155 Hammon Ave., Palm Beach, FL 33480; (561) 655-5430; thecolonypalmbeach.com

One of the four historic hotels of Palm Beach (opened 1947) with lots of charm, located just off Worth Avenue and within easy walking distance to the beach. The building features British Colonial architecture; Floridian shades of salmon-pink, yellow, and emerald-green dominate. Famous for the Royal Room dinner cabaret.

THE CHESTERFIELD PALM BEACH

363 Cocoanut Row, Palm Beach, FL 33480; (561) 659-5800; chesterfieldpb.com

One of the four historic hotels in Palm Beach (opened in 1926), this luxury boutique hotel is situated in the heart of midtown Palm Beach, near to Worth Avenue and 3 blocks back from the beach.

THE BRAZILIAN COURT

301 Australian Ave., Palm Beach, FL 33480; (561) 655-7740; thebraziliancourt.com

One of the four historic hotels of Palm Beach (opened in 1926), a luxury boutique property famous for the Mediterranean Revival architecture and romantic courtyards. Located within 2 blocks of Worth Avenue and 2 blocks back from the beach. Great location.

FOUR SEASONS RESORT PALM BEACH

2800 S. Ocean Blvd., Palm Beach, FL 33480; (561) 582-2800; fourseasons.com/palmbeach

Located toward the southern end of the town of Palm Beach (near the Lake Worth Casino Beach), this is a highly regarded exclusive resort located directly on the ocean with private beach access. The Atlantic Bar & Grill is a great tip for dining directly in the dunes at the beach.

TIDELINE OCEAN RESORT & SPA PALM BEACH

2842 S. Ocean Blvd., Palm Beach, FL 33480; (561) 540-6440; tidelineresort.com

Located toward the southern end of the town of Palm Beach (near the Lake Worth Casino Beach), this is a very contemporary, luxury resort located directly on the ocean with private beach access.

THE EAU PALM BEACH RESORT & SPA

100 S. Ocean Blvd., Manalapan, FL 33462; (561) 533-6000; eaupalmbeach.com

Located toward the southern end of Palm Beach Island in the exclusive coastal town of Manalapan, this oceanfront deluxe resort is particularly notable for its elaborate spa and spectacular ocean bar and restaurant.

THE BRADLEY PARK HOTEL

280 Sunset Ave., Palm Beach, FL 33480; (561) 832-7050; thebradleyparkhotel.com

Ideally located just off Royal Poinciana Way, this historically landmarked 1920s Mediterranean Revival boutique hotel exudes old Palm Beach charm. Many rooms include kitchenettes.

PALM BEACH HISTORIC INN

365 S. County Rd., Palm Beach, FL 33480; (561) 832-4009; palmbeachhistoricinn.com

Located directly at Town Square, this quaint, affordable bed and breakfast boasts a central location 1 block off the ocean. Accommodations are pet friendly and offered with a continental breakfast.

City of West Palm Beach (Across the Bridge from Palm Beach Island)

HILTON WEST PALM BEACH

600 Okeechobee Blvd., West Palm Beach, FL 33401; (561) 231-6000; hilton.com

The top-rated luxury hotel in downtown West Palm Beach, with an expansive pool deck, is within walking distance to CityPlace, Kravis Center for the Performing Arts, and next to the Palm Beach County Convention Center.

WEST PALM BEACH MARRIOTT

1001 Okeechobee Blvd., West Palm Beach, FL 33401; (561) 833-1234; marriott.com

Highly regarded and completely renovated hotel within walking distance to everything in downtown West Palm Beach.

HYATT PLACE WEST PALM BEACH

295 Lakeview Ave., West Palm Beach, FL 33401; (561) 655-1454; hyatt.com

Located right in the center of downtown, within walking distance to everything in downtown West Palm Beach.

RESIDENCE INN BY MARRIOTT

455 Hibiscus St., West Palm Beach, FL 33401; (561) 653-8100; marriott.com

Located directly in the center of downtown West Palm Beach, with an outdoor pool.

GRANDVIEW GARDENS BED & BREAKFAST

1608 Lake Ave., West Palm Beach, FL 33401; (561) 833-9023; grandview-gardens.com

Featuring outside private entrances for all guest suites and balconies or terraces facing the pool, this is one of the top-rated boutique bed and breakfast resorts in the Palm Beach area, located in the Grandview Heights Historic District and within walking distance to all the major sites in downtown West Palm Beach.

CASA GRANDVIEW HISTORIC LUXURY INN COTTAGES & SUITES

1410 Georgia Ave., West Palm Beach, FL 33401; (561) 655-8932; casagrandview.com

Exclusive, highly rated, charming boutique resort (breakfast only) located in the Grandview Heights Historic District adjacent to downtown West Palm Beach, also within walking distance to all the major sites.

PALM BEACH HIBISCUS BED & BREAKFAST

213 S. Rosemary Ave., West Palm Beach, FL 33401; (561) 833-8171; palmbeachhibiscus.com

Upscale bed and breakfast within two historic houses in the heart of downtown featuring a patio bar. Walk to everything.

PALM BEACH VACATION RENTALS

1608 Lake Ave., West Palm Beach, FL 33401; (561) 801-0164; palmbeachvacationrentals.net

Offering a collection of upscale boutique-style fully furnished and equipped vacation homes and apartments in the heart of West Palm Beach.

Palm Beach Gardens, Jupiter & Singer Island (North Palm Beach County)

PGA NATIONAL RESORT & SPA

400 Ave. of the Champions, Palm Beach Gardens, FL 33418; (561) 627-2000; pgaresort.com

The top-rated golf resort in the Palm Beach area with a highly acclaimed spa. Also offering vacation homes.

JUPITER BEACH RESORT & SPA

5 N. A1A, Jupiter, FL 33477; (561) 746-2511; jupiterbeachresort.com

This is a highly rated luxury resort hotel directly on the ocean.

WYNDHAM GRAND JUPITER AT HARBOURSIDE PLACE

122 Soundings Ave., Jupiter, FL 33477; (561) 273-6600; wyndhamgrandjupiter.com

A waterfront luxury hotel situated in the mixed-use Harbourside Place complex.

PALM BEACH MARRIOTT SINGER ISLAND BEACH RESORT & SPA

3800 N. Ocean Dr., Singer Island, Riviera Beach, FL 33404; (561) 340-1700; marriott.com

Large-scale luxury resort and spa directly on the ocean. Also offers fully furnished apartments for short stays.

SAILFISH MARINA RESORT

98 Lake Dr., Palm Beach Shores, FL 33404; (561) 844-1724; sailfishmarina.com

Charming boutique resort with a marina located near the southern tip of Singer Island on the water. Located near the Lake Worth Inlet across from the northern tip of Palm Beach Island, the sprawling compound also features an excellent seafood restaurant directly on the water with spectacular sunset views. Boat dockage also available as well as charter boat services and local boat tours.

Boca Raton & Delray Beach (South Palm Beach County)

BOCA RATON RESORT & CLUB
501 E. Camino Real, Boca Raton, FL 33432; (561) 447-3000; bocaresort.com

One of the most highly rated resorts in Florida and the most exclusive hotel in Boca Raton, this historic sprawling resort boasts an outstanding spa and beachfront complex.

WATERSTONE RESORT & MARINA
999 E. Camino Real, Boca Raton, FL 33432; (561) 368-9500; curiocollection3.hilton.com

Part of the Curio Collection by Hilton, this hotel is located directly on the water with marina docking facilities.

DELRAY BEACH MARRIOTT
10 N. Ocean Blvd., Delray Beach, FL 33483; (561) 274-3200; marriott.com

Great location, facing the ocean on one side and the popular Atlantic Avenue on the other.

THE SEAGATE HOTEL & SPA
1000 E. Atlantic Ave., Delray Beach, FL 33483; (561) 655-4800; theseagatehotel.com

Very upscale, boutique hotel and spa on Atlantic Avenue near the beach.

SUNDY HOUSE
106 S. Swinton Ave., Delray Beach, FL 33444; (877) 439-9601; sundyhouse.com

The top-rated boutique inn in Delray Beach, located just off Atlantic Avenue.

CRANES BEACH HOUSE BOUTIQUE HOTEL & LUXURY VILLAS
82 Gleason St., Delray Beach, FL 33483; (561) 278-1700; cranesbeachhouse.com

A charming, mid-price range boutique hotel (with studio apartments), located just off Atlantic Avenue and near the beach.

Religious Services on Palm Beach Island & Vicinity

ROYAL POINCIANA CHAPEL
Historic (founded by Henry Flagler) non-denominational Christian church
60 Cocoanut Row
Palm Beach, FL 33480
(561) 655-4212

EPISCOPAL CHURCH OF BETHESDA-BY-THE-SEA
Historic Episcopal church
141 S. County Rd.
Palm Beach, FL 33480
(561) 655-4554

ST. EDWARD ROMAN CATHOLIC CHURCH
Historic Roman Catholic church
144 N. County Rd.
Palm Beach, FL 33480
(561) 832-0400

ST. ANN CATHOLIC CHURCH
Historic, oldest catholic church in South Florida. President Kennedy attended his last church service here.
310 N. Olive Ave.
West Palm Beach, FL 33401
(561) 832-3757

HOLY TRINITY EPISCOPAL CHURCH
Historic Episcopal church known for its charming Mediterranean Revival architecture.
211 Trinity Place
West Palm Beach, FL 33401
(561) 655-8650

PALM BEACH ORTHODOX SYNAGOGUE
A modern orthodox synagogue welcoming Jews of all ages, backgrounds, and levels of observance
120 N. County Rd.
Palm Beach, FL 33480
(561) 838-9002

TEMPLE BETH EL
Conservative synagogue affiliated with the United Synagogue of Conservative Judaism
2815 N. Flagler Dr.
West Palm Beach, FL 33407
(561) 833-0339

TEMPLE ISRAEL
The only reform synagogue in West Palm Beach
1901 N. Flagler Dr.
West Palm Beach, FL 33407
(561) 833-8421

Resources

DISCOVER THE PALM BEACHES, THE DESTINATION MARKETING ORGANIZATION OF PALM BEACH COUNTY:
thepalmbeaches.com

THE CULTURAL COUNCIL OF PALM BEACH COUNTY:
palmbeachculture.com

PALM BEACH COUNTY SPORTS COMMISSION:
palmbeachsports.com

THE PALM BEACH CHAMBER:
palmbeachchamber.com

THE CHAMBER OF THE PALM BEACHES:
palmbeaches.org

WEST PALM BEACH VISITOR CENTER:
visitpalmbeach.com

THE *PALM BEACH POST*:
(the region's most circulated newspaper)
palmbeachpost.com

THE PALM BEACH DAILY NEWS:
(the newspaper of the town of Palm Beach)
palmbeachdailynews.com

COMPASS COMMUNITY CENTER:
(the region's LGBTQ Community Center)
compassglcc.com

Acknowledgments

The following organizations have been particularly helpful with the production of this book: the town of Palm Beach, the city of West Palm Beach, Palm Beach County Historical Society, Preservation Foundation of Palm Beach, Worth Avenue Association, Henry Morrison Flagler Museum, and the Breakers, Palm Beach.

Special thanks go to Peter Emmerich for his help in compiling the most important points of interest for the thousands of guests welcomed to Grandview Gardens Bed & Breakfast and Palm Beach Vacation Rentals over the last 15 years, Jim Watson for his help with the manuscript preparation, and my mother Jan Weimar for her encouragement and support.

Furthermore, I'd like to acknowledge the help and support of these individuals: Jed Lyons, Missy Janes, Steven Stolman, Jorge Pesquera, Friederike Mittner, Anka Palitz, David Scott, Scott Simmons, Elizabeth Kuhnke, Debi Murray, Scott Moses, Scott Horne, Rip Jackson, Kay Moss, Chris Brown, Bill Proctor, AJ Wasson, Amanda Skier, Shannon O'Malley, Kirby Kooluris, Tracy Kamerer, Rob Russell, Jason Arbuckle, Ed Schmidt, Bernd Reinheimer, Mitra Esmailzadeh, Shannon Donnelly, Sanda Lambert, Mario Lombardo, Michael Ridgdill, Bill FeldKamp, James Girouard, and Mason Phelps.

Author Rick Rose, left, pictured with his mother Jan Weimar and business partner Peter Emmerich.

INDEX

NOTES

Discover the Palm Beaches (DTPB); thepalmbeaches.com

Cocks, Catherine (2001), *Doing the Town: The Rise of Urban Tourism in the United States, 1850-1915*, University of California Press, pp. 6–7.

palmbeachdailynews.com/news/news/
palm-beachs-33480-ranked-as-nations-richest-zip-co/nMFBc/

Orr, Christina, *Addison Mizner Architect of Dreams and Realities* (Stuart, Florida: Southeastern Printing Company, Inc., 1977), p. 18.

townofpalmbeach.com/index.aspx?NID=343

Orr, Christina, *Addison Mizner Architect of Dreams and Realities* (Stuart, Florida: Southeastern Printing Company, Inc., 1977), p. 20.

Ibid., p 5.

Earl, Polly Anne, *Palm Beach—The Way We Were* (The Preservation Foundation of Palm Beach).

seatemperature.org

weather.com

Note: Ms. Christina Orr's research and publication of *Addison Mizner Architect of Dreams and Realities* was made possible through grants from the Fine Arts Council of Florida and the National Endowment for the Arts. This author feels the book portrays an accurate picture of the architect and has relied on the information provided by the publication.

ABOUT THE AUTHOR

A second-generation Floridian born and raised in the Palm Beach area, Heinrich (Rick) Rose graduated from the Florida State University College of Business with a degree in hospitality management. Rick worked for major hotel groups for 20 years, mainly in distribution and international sales and marketing, based both in the United States and Europe.

Since leaving the international hotel business, Rick co-owns and operates Grandview Gardens Bed & Breakfast and Palm Beach Vacation Rentals in West Palm Beach. After opening the B&B, he was perplexed to learn that many European guests didn't know much about Palm Beach and often confused the famous resort town with Palm Springs, California, so with the help of a friend, the late, local, legendary Florida historian Jim Ponce, Rick put together a tour for B&B guests so they could learn about local history and see the most important points of interest.

The tours became amazingly popular, and subsequently Rick developed a passion for local history, becoming Jim's understudy for Worth Avenue history and, eventually, the historian for the Worth Avenue Association. Today, an active member of the Historical Society of Palm Beach County, the Flagler Museum, and the Palm Beach Preservation Foundation, Rick also was appointed by the Palm Beach County Board of Commissioners to serve on the Board of Directors of Discover the Palm Beaches, Palm Beach County's destination marketing organization.

In addition to leading roughly 2,000 visitors a year on public and private tours of Worth Avenue and Palm Beach Island, Rick welcomes more than 1,900 guests a year to his boutique inn, assisting and helping guests experience the Palm Beaches to the fullest, and solidifying his role as the local insider about all things "Palm Beach."

Rick Rose has put together an invaluable guide to all that is Palm Beach. Don't miss his magical Worth Avenue walking tours. No one does it better than Rick, and he's a snazzy dresser too!

—MARLEY HERRING
President, Worth Avenue Association

I believe that Rick Rose may have lived in Palm Beach in the Gilded Age in another life. Rick's historic perspectives are not only accurate in detail, but peppered with all sorts of juicy tidbits along the way. The weekly tours of Worth Avenue that he conducts for our organization are so much fun and so informative that many people attend time and time again. Rick is a treasure.

—ROBIN MILLER
General Manager, Worth Avenue Association

As a local native born resident, international hotelier, innkeeper, community activist, historian, Worth Avenue tour guide and Palm Beach enthusiast, Rick Rose is highly qualified to author a must-read guide to Palm Beach for visitors and residents alike.

—LAUREL BAKER
Executive Director, Palm Beach Chamber of Commerce